My Twenty Years
· in
Buckingham Palace

A Book of Intimate Memoirs

by

F. J. CORBITT

FORMERLY DEPUTY COMPTROLLER OF SUPPLY
AT BUCKINGHAM PALACE

DAVID McKAY COMPANY, INC.

New York

MANUFACTURED IN THE UNITED STATES OF AMERICA

Van Rees Press. New York

Contents

CHAPTER   PAGE

1   I Join the Royal Staff   3

2   Occasions of State   19

3   Three Royal Weddings   37

4   Catering for Celebrations   44

5   Racing at Cowes and Ascot   50

6   How Buckingham Palace Works   57

7   Balmoral Days and Tales   105

8   When Royalty Celebrates Christmases and Birthdays   121

9   The King in War   145

10   Four Reigns   175

11   Edward the King   213

12   Another Royal Romance: Princess Margaret and Peter Townsend   228

13   The Ever-Changing, Ever-Stable Monarchy   241

MY TWENTY YEARS
IN
BUCKINGHAM PALACE

CHAPTER ONE

I Join the Royal Staff

IT WAS nearly midnight when the telephone rang.

I lifted the receiver and said, a little wearily, "Good evening, Hotel de Paris, Bray, at your service," for this was toward the end of a long spell of night duty, and I was not perhaps as keen and eager to take reservations of rooms or to arrange welcome for late arrivals as I might have been.

But the voice on the telephone was a familiar one—that of my friend, and up to a few months ago, immediate boss, Les Bentley.

"Would you like a job at Buckingham Palace?" he asked.

I must, I thought, be dreaming. I knew very well that Ben had left us at Bray to take up a post on the household staff at the Palace and that he was now working for King George V, but to imagine myself, a twenty-one-year-old night receptionist at this Berkshire hotel, suddenly transferred to Buckingham Palace, the home of the King and Queen, to work there, was beyond possibility. This was in 1932, and Royalty in those days was far more distant and awe-inspiring than in these days, when radio, television, and the films have made us all much more familiar with kings and queens as ordinary human beings instead of special people of a different kind, living in a world of their own, remote from ordinary everyday existence, and unapproachable by anyone like me.

Pulling myself together, I asked Ben to repeat his words. With some impatience in his voice, he asked again, "Would you like a job here at Buckingham Palace?" this time explaining: "We want a man in the office, and I think it is the job for you. Think it over, and I will ring you up again tomorrow night for your answer. Now, good night."

For the rest of that night there was a very wide-awake receptionist on duty at the Hotel de Paris, though his mind was not entirely on his work. It was the magic phrase "Buckingham Palace" that kept ringing through my brain as the small hours passed, more slowly that night than ever before. In the years to come, those two words were to be more familiar to me than any others, but then they still had an awe-inspiring, almost frightening sound.

Here was I, Frederick John Corbitt, ex-office boy in a St. Paul's Churchyard shipping company, ex-elementary schoolboy from Walthamstow, being offered a job within the King's home. It did not seem possible at all, and when I went to my little room on the top floor for my customary few hours' sleep, it was a long time before I could stop worrying about what my answer should be. Next evening I was still undecided. Suppose I failed and let Bentley down, and found myself out of a job altogether? It seemed all too likely. Then I thought of how proud my Scots-born mother, whose family had farmed in Perthshire for generations, and my father, ex-riding master of the 11th Hussars and now a refrigeration engineer, would be to hear their Freddie was working at Buckingham Palace. My mind was made up. I would say, "yes," and try my hardest.

But when the call came, again a little before midnight, my courage oozed. Good friend that he was, Ben sensed my hesitancy through the telephone wires, but would have none of it. "Come up and have lunch at the Palace on your day off

4

next week," he urged. "That won't commit you to anything, and I'll promise you a good lunch."

So it was that, feeling very small, frightened, and alone, I found myself four days later nervously pacing the pavement of Buckingham Palace Road, glancing at the forbidding walls of the Palace, wondering how I could summon up courage to tell the policeman at the gates that I had an appointment with His Majesty's Comptroller of Supply.

Looking back, I have often smiled since at my youthful nerves. But often in later years, when I had to interview candidates for jobs on the staff, and found them so nervous that sometimes they could scarcely speak, I was able to make allowances, and to put them at ease, recalling my own first visit to the Palace.

Eventually, with a sickly feeling in my stomach, I approached the constable at the massive black iron gate, surmounted with a Royal Crown in gold. What if he did not believe me? But as soon as I mentioned my name and business, he smiled and nodded. "That's right," he said, after glancing at a card with a list of names and times on it which he took from his tunic pocket. "Go right ahead, across the forecourt to the door there on the right."

Mumbling some words of thanks, I walked forward in a sort of daze. The first obstacle was overcome; perhaps the others would be just as easy. I did not know then that every day a complete list of callers expected at the Palace is given to the police on duty, with the times of appointments and the names of whatever officials the callers are to see. If your name is on the list, it is open sesame to the gates. If, by any chance—and sometimes things do go wrong, even at the Palace—it has been left off, you will be asked to wait while the constable telephones from the gate to the official concerned for confirmation that you are expected. If no confirmation is forthcoming, you will have to do some high-powered explaining, for unexpected callers and would-be gate-crashers are not welcome at Buckingham Palace.

At the door, which I subsequently learned is known as the Visitors' Door, because it is here that the Royal Visitors' Book, signed by all important callers, is kept, I was greeted by a smiling, elderly man in gorgeous blue-and-gold livery, with a white collar and bow tie, snow-white hair and friendly blue eyes. He was what was then known as a Gentleman-Porter, a rank of upper-servant which has disappeared from the Royal Household since the war. When he heard my name and mission, he, too, consulted a card of names. (They believe in double-checking everything at the Palace.) Then he handed me on to another gorgeously dressed man, this time in red and gold, who led me along a red-carpeted corridor to a gold-and-black lift which took us gently up to the first floor. Here I had a confused impression of white walls with gold decorations, statues and busts in marble, and big oil paintings hanging on the walls, before we came to a white door which bore in the center a printed card with the name Sir Derek Keppel, Master of the Household.

The footman (or rather livery porter, to give him his correct designation) knocked, opened the door, and announced my name.

Behind a wide-topped desk I saw a tall man in black frock coat, high collar, and superbly creased trousers. He wore a white military-style mustache, and immediately he spoke, I knew this was someone used to authority. Indeed, he was, for the Master is responsible for the whole of the domestic staff of the Palace, engages or dismisses servants, and bears the ultimate responsibility for the smooth running and orderly maintenance of the whole of the Palace. It is a job calling for the highest qualities of tact, discipline, and efficiency, and

Sir Derek, as I was to find, combined all these qualities in a remarkable degree, together with the most courtly manners, and a friendly charm which could quickly turn to intimidating anger at the smallest slip or breach of rules. King George V and Queen Mary, as I shall tell you farther on, were much more remote even from members of their own Household than King George VI and Queen Elizabeth, or our present Queen, but Sir Derek was an old family friend, on closer terms with the King and Queen than most of his colleagues.

I knew nothing of this as I stood there, waiting for Sir Derek to speak.

"Sit down and tell me all about yourself," he said, and, feeling more at ease, I launched into a quick account of my career, stressing, as Bentley had warned me to do, my office experience, and my responsibilities as night duty man at the Bray hotel. Sir Derek listened, as he must have done to hundreds of other hopefuls wanting jobs at the Palace, and when I had finished, he rose, nodded, and said, "We will let you know."

What this meant I had no idea. There was nothing to tell me if I had made a good impression or a bad one, but I noticed, as I murmured my thanks and made for the door, another shortish, square-built man who had been sitting in the shadow. He seemed to be smiling at me, and I guessed this was Mr. Harry Mercer, the Comptroller of Supply, Bentley's chief, and the man for whom I would be working if I landed the job. When I found my way to the door, the red-coated servant told me, "Mr. Mercer wants to see you in his office. I will take you round."

Then began what seemed a fantastic, Alice-in-Wonderland sort of adventure, which in later days I used to delight in giving to my friends on their first visit to the Palace. Through a door in the wall my liveried conductor led me into another world. The beautifully kept white plaster and gold walls gave place to walls of rough stone, the floor lost its rich crimson carpet for a surface of bare stone, light came from naked electric bulbs instead of the frosted glass bowls I had admired at the Visitors' Door, with daylight seeping in through occasional iron-barred windows set deep in the eight-feet-thick walls.

Seeing my look of astonishment, my guide smiled. "We're underground now," he explained, after we had gone down a steep, narrow flight of stairs. "You are in the working part of the Palace—behind the scenes, you might say."

In fact, ever afterward I felt it really was just like going behind the scenes at a big theater, to leave the glittering pomp and magnificence of the upper Palace for the workaday, rough-and-ready plainness of the servants' side, in the rooms and corridors where men and women work and move about their business as they might in a factory or a hotel, without a thought that their workplace is a Palace.

After what seemed to me to be an interminable walk through a bewildering succession of stone-flagged corridors, each exactly like the last, we emerged at the head of a flight of stairs in a big square hall, about which several men and women—some of the men in livery, some not—were moving purposefully, carrying trays, piles of linen, decanters, and other household items. This, at least, was familiar territory. It was just like backstairs at the Hotel de Paris, and I had begun to feel at home before my guide opened a door marked with a card similar to that I had seen upstairs, "Comptroller of Supply," and ushered me into a room where, to my delight, the familiar figure of Bentley was awaiting me.

"How did you get on? Have a glass of sherry? Harry will be along in a minute," said my friend, all in one breath, and before I had time to reply, he had poured out one of the largest sherries I had ever seen and offered it to me.

He caught my look of surprise. "That's what we call a Royal," he explained. "In honor of your first visit, you see."

I examined the glass, which was one of those lovely cut-glass wine goblets specially made for Palace use, bearing the Sovereign's cipher, G.R.V., and a crown above the fluting. They hold considerably more than an ordinary sherry glass. In those free-and-easy days, with sherry, bottled in the Royal cellars at St. James's Palace, at 3s. 6d. a bottle, and whisky plentiful at 10s. 6d., the Royal servants and staff could—and did—do themselves very well. There was no excess, but neither was there any skimping.

Now the door opened and in came the man I had guessed as Mr. Mercer. "Well, young fellow, you made a good start. Sir Derek likes your manner, and I think you'll get on well," he said, giving me a warm handshake. "Now let's have some lunch."

The three of us sat down at a round table in the next room, beautifully laid with spotless white linen and gleaming cutlery, while a black-liveried servant, quite a youth, served us with an excellent meal of soup, roast veal and vegetables, a sweet and some Stilton cheese, accompanied by a good white wine.

It was a delightful introduction to a new job, and, warmed by the sherry and the white wine, I felt expansive and confident. Harry Mercer, who afterward became a close and dear friend as well as my chief for many years, was an excellent host. All my fears and timidity had disappeared, for I felt I was among friends, and walked out of the Tradesmen's Entrance feeling a very different and much more confident young man than when I walked in. Buckingham Palace was, as I soon found out, a delightful place to work in those far-off days of plenty. Everyone, from the noblemen and ladies of title who formed the circle round the King and Queen, to the humblest of their domestic staff, was proud to be in the Royal service, and each, in greater or less degree, enjoyed the lavishness of life in a house where money still was not a problem. When I had been there a few months, I found out that even this spacious way of doing things was "nothing like it used to be." It was true that, as a result of recommendations made by a Government Committee under the late Sir George (later Lord) May, King George V, to set an example to the nation, had cut down much of his personal expenditure and ordered that there should be a general tightening-up of Palace expenses. Lots of old customs, like the provision of a bottle of whisky every night for the Royal bedroom, which dated back to the days of the early Georges, had been abolished before I arrived on the staff. (That bottle of whisky had been regarded as one of the perquisites of the King's Page, and that worthy was most irate when his supplies were cut off.) But the staff of those days could never have imagined the scaling-down of Royal ways that I was to witness in my nineteen years in the Household. They grumbled, just the same, and all through my time at the Palace I heard the same old theme repeated by the older servants year by year, "It's nothing like it used to be."

All this was in the unknown future as I made my way back to Bray to take up my night duties again. That night my new confidence soon evaporated, and I was frankly frightened at what I had done. All the doubts about being able to cope with Royalty, to keep my end up in the Palace amid all those awe-inspiring men in livery who seemed so proud and disdainful of outsiders, came flooding back, and several times I was on the point of writing to Mr. Mercer to withdraw my name.

Anyway, I comforted myself, maybe I did not make much of an impression and I shall soon have a letter telling me I am

not wanted. But when the letter—a most impressive docu-
ment, headed with the Royal Crown in red, and in an envelope
bearing no postage stamp but the magic frank of the Buckingham Palace post office—arrived a few days later, it brought
the exciting news from Sir Derek Keppel that he had decided,
with the approval of H.M. The King, to take me on for a
trial period of six months, with a permanent position on the
staff if I proved to be satisfactory. Now there was no turning back. I told my mother and father, who were naturally
delighted. My four sisters were very amused. "You won't
stay there long, Freddie," they said. "Wait till Queen Mary
sees you!"

Worried though I was about how I should get on, I did
not think it was as bad as all that. Already at Bray I had
been on nodding terms with lords and ladies, several Indian
maharajahs, and had been at close quarters with one King
and Queen, so I had, I flattered myself, some experience. The
Hotel de Paris at Bray was very smart and fashionable, and
patronized by young members of Society and members of
the theatrical profession. We had many famous visitors for
lunch, dinner, and weekends. Even one member of the Royal
Family, the Prince of Wales, later the Duke of Windsor, was
a fairly frequent guest at the hotel, sometimes staying till
3 A.M. dancing and enjoying a gay party with friends. Film
stars like Cary Grant, Wallace Beery, and Gloria Swanson
would be in the dining room, with some of the gay set from
Mayfair: men like "Jumbo" Joliffe, the Maharajah of Raj-
pipla and actresses like Ruby Miller. King Alfonso of Spain
and his wife, Queen Ena, granddaughter of our own Queen
Victoria, frequently came over on Sundays for lunch, and to
spend the afternoon on the river in a hired motor launch. All
these people were gay, lighthearted, and big spenders in those
days when no one seemed to take life seriously at all, and

the Hotel de Paris was as good a training ground for the bigger, more important world of Buckingham Palace as you could find.

Soon—much too soon for my liking—the fateful day came round, and off I set for the Palace once more. This time my heart was in my mouth again as I confronted those formidable railings, the impassive sentries, the watchful police. But I put on a bold front and marched steadily forward to the constable at the Trade Gate. (I had been told to go in this way, and not through the dignified official Visitors' Door, now that I was starting as a member of the staff.) A minute or two was enough to convince the kindly policeman that I was expected, and I found myself once again in the home of the King of England.

At first it took a bit of realizing. I had forgotten the gloomy, untidy, backstage atmosphere of this part of the Palace, with its unshaded electric-light bulbs glowing yellow high in the lofty ceiling, empty packing cases stacked by the wall, two rolled carpets slung on the stone floor waiting to be taken to the cleaners, and a flight of very worn stone steps leading upward into other mysterious parts of the great house. My red-liveried guide ("Digger," the porter from the Trade Gate, for years a friend of every member of the Royal staff) touched me on the shoulder and led me through a glass-paneled door into the familiar surroundings of Harry Mercer's sitting room and office combined.

Harry was a man of medium height, with a gray mustache, who always wore a high, turned-down, stiff collar and black tie, with a Royal cipher tie pin given him by King Edward VII. He was something of a Victorian in his approach to his job and to life in general, and believed in doing a good day's work, then enjoying relaxation among the good things of life. He was no lover of modern methods of rush and bustle, which he always declared left things skimped, and were in no way suitable for the Palace. I often smile to think what he would say to the up-to-date methods that have been introduced into Buckingham Palace in the past five or six years, especially since the accession of the Queen and the advent of the Duke of Edinburgh, himself the arch-exponent of the use of time-saving devices and gadgets.

It was a warm day in June, and I had only just got used to the Palace surroundings, when my chief told me I was to travel to Windsor right away to help in the preparations for Ascot Week. The King and Queen, with their usual big house party, were going into residence at the Castle that evening, and would be at Windsor for the rest of the week, traveling over each day to the famous course to watch the racing.

After a train journey from London, I found myself walking up Castle Hill and through the archway, past the famous Round Tower, to the Trade Entrance, where a policeman and a servant, in the familiar red-and-gold livery, asked my name and business. When they found I was a "new boy," the servant offered to conduct me to the office of the Comptroller of Supply, and I again walked along underground passages, stone-flagged, as at the Palace, but lighter, with occasional trophies of ancient armor at the side to underline the historical character of this oldest of British Royal homes.

"If you get lost on the way back, someone will turn up to show you the way," said my guide, as he left me at the office door.

Proud of my Boy Scout training, and remembering my experiences at the Palace, I smiled, confident of my ability to retrace my steps at any time. But those Windsor corridors, below ground or above, are equally confusing, and I got completely lost half a dozen times within my first three days at the Castle, before I learned to look for certain landmarks. Even then, it was only a fraction of the vast Castle that I had come to know, and it was many years before I could, with confidence, find my way generally about the maze of corridors, passages, and staircases that honeycomb the ancient fortress-home.

My first real job came during the morning, when I had to write an order for the local tradesmen for crescent rolls, Gressini sticks (a sort of yeastless bread, made of flour and water, for diabetics, which King George V liked to eat with his meals), and Gorgonzola and Brie cheese. This was routine stuff to me, straight from the hotel at Bray, and it was only when I came to write out the next order on a requisition form addressed to the Head Gardener, Windsor Castle, that I realized I was arranging for dinner, or part of it, for the King and Queen, and if I made a slip They (I always spelled it with a capital letter in my mind) would perhaps go without something they particularly wanted. I need not have worried, for there was, and still is, a system of checking by the chef and others which makes mistakes of this kind next to impossible. But when, that evening, I was taken by a kindly Page to see the Royal dining room, with the table laid in readiness for the King and Queen and their guests, it was a great thrill for me to know I had ordered the figs and plums and pears and grapes that were piled high on lovely china dishes on the sideboard.

Since then, of course, I have ordered literally tons of foodstuffs of all kinds for nearly all the members of our Royal Family, and have seen tables laid out for State banquets, wedding breakfasts, and other great occasions. But none of these ever gave me quite the thrill of that first sight of a Royal table I had helped to furnish. Next day much the same sort of thing went on. I found the work fairly easy, so long as I did not let the Royal rank of my new employers overwhelm me. Officials and clerks and servants were most kind, and anxious to help me. By the end of the week I had made several friends, and felt fairly confident about my job.

Ascot Week soon passed, and though I found we were all entitled to special passes for the roof of the Royal Box (where, incidentally, you get perhaps the finest view of racing in all Britain) or to badges for the grandstand and paddock, I did not get a chance of going to the races that year. Next week the Royal Standard flew over Buckingham Palace once again, and I was back in the outer office there, gradually learning the routine from my chief, Harry Mercer, and his assistant—my friend, Les Bentley. Not long after, I learned, we were going north to Edinburgh for a stay at Holyroodhouse, where the King was to give a big garden party and hold other functions. This was exciting news for me. I had never been to Scotland before, and I was getting a little impatient to catch a glimpse of either the King or the Queen, neither of whom I had seen so far, even in the distance. Some of the older under-servants told me they had been at the Palace for two or three years without seeing their Royal employers, but, they assured me, there was much more chance of this when the Court was away from London and Windsor.

I had visions of traveling on that most exclusive of all railway conveyances, the Royal train, but I was speedily disillusioned. Instead, I was to journey north by ordinary night train in advance of the Royal party, my fare paid, of course, by the Privy Purse department through a voucher system which covers all Royal travel. This, incidentally, provided me with my first sidelight on the expenses of Royalty. For the whole Court—the Royal Family, their suites, the minor officials, clerks, servants, detectives, police, and chauffeurs—to go from London to Edinburgh cost in those days about £300 to £350 for fares, and food on the journey, alone.

This was the first of many scores of long- and short-distance rail journeys I made during my years at the Palace. The Court spends a good deal of time as well as money in moving from one place to the other: London to Edinburgh, to Balmoral, to Windsor, to Sandringham, and sometimes farther afield to the Channel Islands, and to Ulster. For tours of the Commonwealth, or travels abroad, a different system operates. A hand-picked band of members of the Household and servants, with the minimum of clerks, go with the Royal travelers, while the greater part of the staff stay at home. This means fairly easy times for those who stay behind, especially if the Royal trip is a long one, but there was always plenty to do. Accounts had to be made up, books checked, stock taken, and so on. But on nearly all the United Kingdom trips, I went off with the advance party, and looked after the supplies for the Royal Family and Household all the time they were away.

Moving the Court is very like a full-scale military operation. Every detail is planned days if not weeks in advance, a circumstance that used to cause us a lot of worry in war days, when security needs had to be weighed up against the necessity for advance arrangements. It always required a good deal of careful thought to arrange for the right members of the staff to travel in advance, to get whichever residence we were making for ready for the Royal arrival, and at the same time not to deprive the Palace of the staff needed to carry on till the King and Queen left. But it always worked out in the end. One thing I soon learned was that my office at the other end was always completely empty till I arrived, which meant all our office equipment, even to pens and ink

16

and blotting pads, had to be taken with us. One or two minor crises taught me not to be absent-minded in this packing process, and I twisted one or two of the old soldiers' phrases for my use.

Instead of muttering "knife, fork, spoon, razor, brush, etc.," I would quietly say to myself, "Dictionary, Kelly's directory, Whittakers, Crockfords," and so on, completing the list of books of reference, diaries, calendars, etc., etc. One of the first and most abiding rules of life with the Royal Family I learned was that there must be no excuses. The King and Queen (and the Queen today) expect everything to be in just as apple-pie order, the service as faultless, their comfort of the same high standard, at Balmoral or Holyroodhouse, or Timbuktu for that matter, if they ever went there, as at home at Buckingham Palace.

My first visit to Scotland is one I shall never forget. The Palace of Holyroodhouse is dark and gloomy inside. The dining rooms and drawing rooms, unused from one Royal visit to the next, usually twelve months later, except when the Monarch's deputy, the Lord High Commissioner for the Church of Scotland, takes up residence for a brief period each year, have, or at least had in those days, an ancient, musty sort of smell. The ancient wooden floors give out odd creaks. My sleeping quarters were up in one of the towers overlooking the Palace forecourt and fountain. Though the nights in this month of July were short, with light until nearly eleven o'clock, I well recall what an eerie business I found it making my way that first night from my office on the ground floor to my room near the roof. My way led me through the famous Darnley Room, where it is said Lord Darnley struck down Rizzio, Court musician and Italian favorite of Mary, Queen of Scots. On the floor is a brass plate recording the deed and the date. I wondered, as I passed, if some ghosts from the past might still haunt this historic spot, and shivered as I heard ominous noises from the creaking floor. But there was nothing more, and reassured, I hurried off to bed—to sleep, I am glad to report, very soundly. From that day on I never worried about having to pass through the murder chamber.

CHAPTER TWO

Occasions of State

IT was one of the greatest privileges of my job at Buckingham Palace to be one of the organizers behind the scenes of many glittering occasions of State, and nearly always an interested and eager, though usually hidden, spectator of them.

The Royal Family have to endure so much staring from the general public, as part of the job they do so tirelessly year in year out, that they resent being stared at in their own homes, especially by members of the staff. So if any of the officials wanted to see what was going on at a Court, a ball, or a dinner party—and naturally we always did—we had to take pretty good care to keep out of the way. In the great State Ballroom, scene of most of the principal State functions at the Palace, there is a wonderful organ, placed there by Queen Victoria for her beloved husband, Albert the Prince Consort, who was a player of no mean skill. Since his day there has been a complete dearth of organ players in the Royal Family, but the great instrument still stands as an imposing feature of the big room, at the opposite end from the Royal dais. Like every organ, this one has a loft, from which you can command a magnificent view of the whole room. In this loft the band is stationed on Court or ball nights, but there is room behind the grill for a few spectators, and it was from this vantage point that I watched many historic scenes in the Court of St. James's, with the pleasant feeling that, in a small way, I had helped to make history, by seeing that everything needed for the entertainment of some important visitor had been provided.

These State scenes are among the most wonderful memories I have of my Palace days, full of color and magnificence, unmatchable in the world. No Hollywood producer, whatever his resources, can ever put such splendor on the screen, for this is the real thing: the jewels of the Queen and her ladies, real and beyond price, the uniforms and Orders of the men supreme with that dignity only the British seem capable of achieving.

With the King of England the central figure in a scene of glowing warmth and stately movement, his Consort, elegantly gowned and wearing a coronet of diamonds, at his side, his courtiers around him in multi-hued uniforms of State, Ambassadors and Ministers of foreign Powers standing grave with responsibility in the circle round the crimson-carpeted dais, with the Royal Arms of England woven on tapestry behind, I remember these occasions as having something of the quality of a painting by one of the old masters, remote from this day of equality and utility.

Of them all, it was the evening Courts which King George V and Queen Mary used to hold together that were the most magnificent, and that made me wish most for the ability of a great artist to record the scenes as they deserved in rich colors and bold design. Now, in these more restricted days, the evening Courts have vanished, probably forever, from the Royal scene; so it is indeed history that I recall in my mind's eye. No one who has not seen an evening Court can have any idea of the British Monarchy at the zenith of its splendor. King George V, resplendent in the scarlet uniform of Colonel-in-Chief of the Guards, the blue ribbon of the Garter across his chest, would sit on a Chair of State on the dais, with Queen Mary, ablaze with diamonds, at his side, his impassive Ghurka aides-de-camp beside him radiating an impression of immense strength and confidence. No woman can ever have worn jewelry with such superb grace as Queen Mary. As she inclined her head in acknowledgment of the debutantes' curtsies, the soft light from the great rose-crystal chandeliers would sparkle in a million flashing points of color from her diamonds and here, you felt, was a Queen indeed, full of majesty, and matchless in her deportment.

I have seen many foreign Sovereigns and their Consorts at the Palace on State visits, accompanied by the bearers of names that have been illustrious in the history of Europe for many centuries, wearing orders and decorations of their native lands. But never have I seen any to compare with our British orders. So many others are too garish, too flamboyant; the colors always seemed to me a little wrong.

The strangest thing about the Palace Courts was that, despite the many colored uniforms, the gold and scarlet of the Gentlemen-at-Arms, with their helmets topped with tall plumes of white swansdown, the crimson and gold and black of the Tudor garb of the Yeomen of the Guard, the glittering full-dress uniforms of the Army officers, the dark and light blue of the Navy and the R.A.F., the somber black knee breeches and silk stockings of the civilian guests, and the rainbow-hued dresses of the women, all seemed to fall into a perfect harmony of color.

One of the most impressive figures in all this gathering of splendor was always the Lord Chamberlain, chief officer of the Court, the man who even today leads Royal processions from the private family apartments of the Palace to the State Rooms walking backward—one of the last few remaining practices of feudal days. On the tail of his Court dress coat, richly embroidered in gold lace, he wears a symbolic golden key, in token of the fact that he has the keys of the King's house and controls all admission thereto. It was to him that fell the duty of announcing the names of the white-gowned debutantes, each with the three tall white Prince of Wales' plumes in her hair, and long white gloves on her hands and arms, as they advanced in turn to make low, sweeping curtsies first to the King, then to the Queen, while the ladies presenting them stood gracefully at the side.

On Court nights there would be upward of two thousand people at the Palace, so security and other precautions were very strictly enforced. To gate-crash a Royal Court was held to be quite impossible, so elaborate was the system of checking names and invitations; yet one year, I recall, there was something like panic behind the scenes when a housemaid reported seeing a strange woman wandering at will through the private rooms of the King and Queen over in the northwest wing. Plain-clothes police hurried off to investigate, and, sure enough, found the uninvited guest. But she was no gate-crasher, merely a lady from a foreign country who, walking out of the ballroom, had lost her way in the corridors, and, unseen by the Pages and other servants, had penetrated into the Royal Family apartments. She was most apologetic and contrite, but somehow most of us never believed it was quite by accident she had found her way to the Royal rooms, especially when it became known later that a discreet police check had revealed a tiny camera in her evening handbag.

Such excitements were rare, but I recall two other incidents that caused much amusement in the Royal entourage. On one Court night, in my early years, a debutante seemed much more overcome by shyness than her sister-debs. Her face was flushed as she waited her turn to go before the thrones.

Officials thought sympathetically that the ordeal (and an ordeal it was indeed) of the long wait in the Mall, where the debs' cars would queue up for two or three hours before the Palace gates were open, with crowds staring in at the occupants all the time, had been too much for her. As her turn to be presented approached, she made an excuse, and was conducted quickly to the ladies' room, where a maid offered her *sal volatile*. This she refused, taking instead a draught from a gold-plated flask she carried in her bag, after which she made her way back to the ballroom, composedly enough, but leaving a strong smell of brandy behind her. She walked out steadily when her name was called, sank into a deep curtsy— but found the effort of rising again a little too much. Officials sprang forward to help her and she was quickly taken to her car and sent home. The draught in the ladies' room had been by no means the first she had taken that evening.

There was always a plentiful supply of champagne in the State Room after the presentations were over, but that was the only case I ever heard of a debutante taking too much before her debut. This incident had a sequel many years later at one of the afternoon Presentation parties which since the war have taken the place as a milk-and-water, or rather tea-and-cakes, substitute for the glories of the evening Courts. At first, debutantes and the ladies presenting them and their escorts were merely invited to a small-scale garden party at the Palace, where the Royal Family walked informally among them, as at the big end-of-the-season garden parties each July. Girls making their debut might only catch a distant glimpse of the Sovereign, and never have the opportunity of making a curtsy at all. But King George VI decided this was not quite good enough, and arranged that the debutantes should pass before the throne in the ballroom before going on to take tea either in the garden or in one of the other State Rooms.

These functions, with the ladies in afternoon gowns and the men in plain morning clothes, have of course nothing like the romantic appeal of the old-style Courts, which I do not think we shall ever see again.

At one of these receptions an Australian girl sank into a most graceful and deep curtsy when her name was announced by the Lord Chamberlain, with the wife of the Australian High Commissioner, who was making the presentations, watching her proudly. But pride turned to consternation when the girl from the Commonwealth did not rise again. The poor girl, in some strange way, had managed to dislocate her knee as she curtsied, and had to be taken from the Palace by ambulance. After this, a general warning to all debutantes not to make exaggerated curtsies was issued— though few ever knew why.

It was at one of the prewar Courts that the most amusing incident of all occurred. A lady of title, famous for her dignified manner, moved across the ballroom floor to greet a friend when she experienced a certain discomfort in her clothing. With admirable presence of mind, she stood still and beckoned three or four of her friends round her. With them acting as a screen, she made herself comfortable by removing the offending garment. Now the only problem remaining was what to do with it (or rather them). But she refused to lose her composure, and advancing majestically to one of the crimson silk covered settees, she sat down and stuffed the garment between the cushions. None of the officials or servants had any idea of what was going on until next morning, when a housemaid went to the office of the Palace Superintendent and produced, with high glee, the pair of silk knickers she had found hidden in the settee.

24

The tale spread through the Palace like wildfire, and there was much speculation about the owner, whom most of us thought would never have the nerve to claim her property. But before the morning had passed, a taxi drew up at the Trade Gate, and a demure lady's maid stepped from it to ask if Lady . . . .'s lingerie had been found.

These unexpected diversions did little if anything to mar the sense of awe that overcame me whenever I peeped at the scene on a Court night. It was all so very like something from Dumas's *Three Musketeers,* and I felt I would never be surprised to see D'Artagnan, or his companions, step forth from behind one of those big, priceless Gobelin tapestries that hang from the walls of the great ballroom. They would have felt quite at home in the Palace atmosphere.

In this ballroom, later on, King George VI and Queen Elizabeth used to give semi-private, semi-official dances, which were some of the best organized and most enjoyable parties in London. A well-known dance band would play, stationed below the organ loft, with a program of foxtrots, waltzes, and rhumbas. The late Mr. Carroll Gibbons was one of King George's favorite band leaders, and many is the time I have taken him from the ballroom into one of the nearby offices to give him a glass of whisky and a sandwich during an interval. With his great reputation and many friends, he was as used as a man can be to flattery and praise, but I have seen his face light up with real pleasure when one of the Pages of the Presence has come to him with a personal message from the King or Queen to say how much they enjoyed the last number. Once, I recall, a Page came hurrying in, almost breathless.

"Princess Elizabeth wants you to play such and such a number next time," he said.

Carroll Gibbons, for the moment, looked worried. "I wonder where she has heard that one?" he asked.

I told him that the Princess probably knew it from some of the American records which friends of hers in the States sent over to her, enabling her to hear certain dance tunes long before anyone else in London knew of them. This was indeed the case with this particular tune, and what worried Carroll was the fact that his band did not know the parts. But this was a Royal request, not lightly to be disregarded. So with a hurried good-by Carroll Gibbons left me and went back to his post; I followed, curious to see what would happen. After a rapid consultation with his band, Carroll Gibbons sat down at the piano with only his leading saxophonist at his side. In a moment or two the ballroom was filled with the haunting strains of this particular tune, played on the piano perfectly by Carroll Gibbons purely from memory, with the saxophonist taking up the tune in a delightful way. After this number another message came to us behind the scenes, again from Princess Elizabeth. It was of cordial thanks to Carroll Gibbons for gratifying her wish.

During the war, of course, State ceremonials and pageantry were at a discount. For one thing, all the State liveries and all the full-dress uniforms had been put into storage for the duration. For another, people were too busy fighting the battle for freedom to worry much about ceremonial. But nevertheless a certain amount of ceremonial life at Buckingham Palace did go on. Of all the functions at the Palace during the war, it was the Investitures which the King held once a week which topped the list for ceremonial grandeur. Despite the wartime simplicity of the uniforms worn by the King, the officials in attendance upon him, and by the men and women attending the Investitures to receive their medals and decorations on Tuesday mornings, there was nevertheless something enormously impressive about those functions.

At the beginning of the war the King held one or two Investitures in the open air, following the example of his father. But as the war took on stern reality and as the list of honors and decorations grew longer every day, it was obvious that something more positive would have to be done to cope with the increasing flow of those entitled to receive their decorations at their Sovereign's hand. Suggestions, I believe, were made to the King that he should delegate this duty either to some members of his family, or to some of the Commanding Officers in the various theaters of war. To all these suggestions the King, already overburdened with the enormous pressure of State duties and wartime audiences, replied with a decisive, "No."

The Sovereign, he firmly maintained, is the fount of all honor in this country. He therefore took it as an essential part of his Royal duties that when his subjects were to be honored, they should receive the honor direct from him, and not from any intermediary. This involved a really enormous amount of work for the King. It was both a physical and a mental strain, receiving as he did perhaps two hundred and fifty, or even in some cases three hundred and fifty, men and women during the course of a morning, and decorating each one of them, as well as shaking each by the hand and having a few brief words of conversation.

These functions took place in the Grand Hall on the ground floor. For one reason, this enabled access to the air-raid shelters to be gained more readily in case of need. For another, the first floor of the Palace, where the State Rooms are situated, was declared "out of bounds" for the duration. This was purely a precautionary measure, but it embraced the King and the Queen themselves, for in normal times their private apartments were situated, as the present Queen's are today, on the first floor of the Palace in the northwest wing. Fortunately there was never any occasion on which those attending an Investiture had to go down to the air-raid shelters during the bombing. But several times we had the "purple" warning, meaning that air-raiders were approaching. Anxiously, the Royal Household officials would survey the scene. Colonel Sir Piers Legh, the Master of the Household, would walk around to make sure that the gangways and passages leading to the air-raid shelters were free of access. But each time the "purple" passed off and the raiders did not come within our immediate vicinity. Once, however, in the days of the flying bombs, the police insisted on the King and his guests taking cover, and half a dozen Knights alive today can claim they were "dubbed" in the Royal air-raid shelter.

In the Grand Hall a dais was set up just outside the entrance to the Bow Room, which is one of the most famous and best-known apartments at Buckingham Palace. It is through this room that the thousands of visitors to the Royal Garden Party in July pass on their way to the gardens from the grand entrance. The recipients of honors, each of whom was allowed, by the King's special permission, to bring two guests with him or her to see the ceremony, were lined up in order of precedence in the Household breakfast room. This order of precedence was based not on military rank or title, but on the degree of the honor or decoration which had been won. So you found a private who had won the Victoria Cross taking precedence of two Generals, an Admiral, and a R.A.F. Marshal, each of whom was to be decorated with the Grand Cross of the Order of the Bath.

After the King had instituted the George Cross, recipients of this honor also took precedence over everyone else except the V.C.'s. Formed up in a long line of bravery, the men and

28

women awaited the King's arrival in the Grand Hall. As His Majesty walked in, accompanied by three or four members of his Household in uniform, one of them carrying a red velvet cushion, the band stationed in the well of the Grand Hall played the National Anthem. It was a moving sight as all the brave men and women came stiffly to attention and saluted their Sovereign, while their friends sitting in the Grand Hall rose. Then the King in a clear voice would say, "Please be seated." The guests would sit down, the Lord Chamberlain announce the name of the first hero or heroine to be decorated, and so the long ceremony of the Investiture would begin.

I recall one, but only one, occasion when it was a woman who led the whole line of those to be decorated. This was Odette Churchill, who suffered so greatly at the hands of the Gestapo after she had been captured when working with the French resistance in France. Odette was awarded the George Cross, and the King told her, as he gave her the coveted medal, that it had rarely given him more pleasure to bestow a decoration. In the case of winners of the Victoria Cross and the George Cross, the Lord Chamberlain read out the citation of the deed for which they had been awarded the decoration. The most remarkable tales of heroism in the war were told in the dry, sometimes stilted words of these official accounts, but sometimes the Earl of Clarendon (then Lord Chamberlain) would pause, his voice trembling a little with emotion, as he recounted the stories of these valiant deeds.

One by one the heroes and heroines marched smartly forward and came to attention in front of the King. From the red velvet cushion held by a member of the Household, the King would take the appropriate medal or decoration and hand it to the recipient. He actually hung the medals on the small hook which had been placed on the left breast of the recipient's tunic. The greatest care was taken by the officials of the Lord Chamberlain's department that the medals and decorations should not get out of order. If anyone fell out of the list of those to be given decorations, as often happened for one reason or another, there was a hurried re-arrangement of the medals, and a checking five minutes before the King came into the room. But it was the proud boast of Lord Clarendon and his officials that never once throughout the whole series of Investitures, at which, I believe, the King decorated something like sixty-five thousand men and women, was there a case of anyone being given the wrong decoration—a wonderful record.

The King thoroughly enjoyed these ceremonies and liked meeting the men and women who were serving him so well. Nor were those heroes who had died while winning their awards, or who subsequently had been killed, forgotten. The King ordered special arrangements to be made in these cases where the next-of-kin of the dead man or woman could come to Buckingham Palace to receive the award from His Majesty's own hand.

These next-of-kin—sometimes an elderly father, sometimes a small boy who was the son of the dead hero—came to the Palace, each accompanied by relatives or friends. They would be taken into a private room away from the Grand Hall, where the King would see them and talk to them in privacy before the ceremony of the Investiture began. Often on these occasions the King was extremely moved by the sad stories he had heard before he came in to take his place on the dais.

In 1943 so great was the pressure of those waiting to receive medals and awards from the King that for some time two Investitures a week instead of one had to be held, one on Tuesday and one on Friday. As a result of doing this double work,

by the end of the war there was not a very big list left over
to deal with. But even so it was found impossible for the King
to present every award, and reluctantly he had to agree to
issue an ordinance that decorations like the M.B.E. (Member
[of the Order] of the British Empire), and a few others of a
similar kind, would be sent to the recipients by registered
post. This was very disappointing for the men and women
who had gained these decorations, but it was unavoidable.

When the King was away visiting his troops in Italy and
North Africa, the Queen had to deputize for him as one of
the Councilors of State. The question then arose, Should the
Investitures be suspended while the King was away, or what
should be done? Queen Elizabeth solved this problem in her
own characteristic manner. She suggested to the King that
she should take his place. He readily agreed, as he almost
always did to suggestions from his wife, and for the first time
since the death of Queen Victoria in 1901, medals and decorations were given out at an Investiture at Buckingham Palace
by a Queen.

I remember the story of one Brigadier who was awarded a
certain class of the Order of the Bath. He came to the Investiture which the Queen held while the King was in Italy in 1944.
His delight at receiving his decoration from the Queen was
enormous. "I shall treasure this to my dying day," I heard
him declare afterward. But the story of his bravery was not
yet complete. He went back to the war and was awarded a
higher class of the Order of the Bath. It is a rule of the Orders
of Chivalry that if you are promoted in them you must return
the insignia of the lower rank when you are given the insignia
of the higher one.

Now the turn of the Brigadier to revisit Buckinham Palace
to receive the insignia of the higher class of the Order of the
Bath came. When he came to their table with the collar of the

order showing his higher rank in it round his neck, officials of the Lord Chamberlain's department asked him where the insignia of his lower order was.

"I've lost it," declared the Brigadier, with a twinkle in his eye.

Officials warned him that he would have to pay the value of the missing insignia. The Brigadier replied that he could not care less how much it cost him.

"That insignia was given me by Her Majesty the Queen," he told the officials. "I would not part with that for all the money in the world."

Later, the story of the Brigadier and his reluctance to part with the insignia given him by the Queen was told to the King and Queen. I believe Queen Elizabeth regarded it as one of the greatest and most touching compliments she had ever been paid.

The first big-scale Royal ceremony in which I took any active part was the Silver Jubilee of King George V, in 1935. January and February of that year were spent as usual at Sandringham. The King was in the best of spirits and seemed to have recovered entirely from the heaviest strain he had ever endured since his severe illness in 1928. Actually this was only an outward appearance. In reality the King's health was not good, though none of us, even those of his servants who came into daily and close contact with him, realized that there was anything fundamentally wrong. He was out with the guns every day as usual, and seemed thoroughly to enjoy his holiday in Norfolk. Then the King was advised by his doctors to take the sea air again. This time he went to Compton Place, the Duke of Devonshire's house at Eastbourne, which the Duke lent to his friend and Sovereign. From Eastbourne we traveled back to Windsor Castle for Easter. There was the usual large house party and the usual Eastertide festivities, in which the King's little grandchildren, our present Queen and Princess Margaret, joined with great glee, bringing a ray of sunshine to gladden their grandfather's heart.

No one ever saw King George V happier or gayer than when he was playing with his two grandchildren, who always referred to him, affectionately, as "Grandpapa England," much to his delight.

Preparations for the Silver Jubilee festivities were going ahead speedily. Plans were made for celebrations at Buckingham Palace, and for drives round London. No one at Windsor Castle, including King George V and Queen Mary, however, had any idea of the great burst of popular enthusiasm, the great demonstration of love, affection, and loyalty, which were to greet the King and Queen on the anniversary of their accession day, May 6. The Court returned to London a few days before the anniversary. As usual, the moment the King's car drew out of the Castle Gates the Royal Standard flying over the Round Tower was hauled down, to be replaced by the Union Jack. Whenever the Royal Standard is flying over Windsor Castle it means that the Sovereign is staying within, but when the Sovereign is not at the Castle, it is the Union Jack which flies over the Round Tower. (In the reign of King George VI there was an exception to this rule. When the King and Queen were spending the weekend quietly at their own country house, Royal Lodge, in Windsor Great Park, a few miles from the castle, the King gave orders that his Standard should still fly over the Castle. The reason for this was that Royal Lodge was completely private. The King did not wish to advertise his presence there to anyone, even by flying his Standard from the roof. So, as he was within the precincts of Windsor Castle, he had the Standard flown from the Castle itself, instead of from the house where he was actually staying.)

On the morning of Silver Jubilee Day, King George V came down into the Grand Hall, an impressive figure in the full-dress scarlet uniform of a Field Marshal, with the blue ribbon of the Garter across his chest. With him was Queen Mary, radiant and regal and with an air of indefinable majesty. As they took their places in the open State landau to drive to St. Paul's Cathedral for the thanksgiving service for the twenty-five years of their reign, with the scarlet-clad footmen climbing into position behind them, their white breeches gleaming in the pale May sunshine, and the outriders in their blue jockey-caps and scarlet-and-gold tunics escorting the State landau, I thought it was a thrilling sight.

All of us on the Royal staff were allowed to bring guests into the Palace, and we hurried into the forecourt to watch the King and Queen drive out, accompanied by a Sovereign's Escort of the Household Cavalry. When the Royal party returned from St. Paul's there was a big luncheon at which all members of the Royal Family were present. They pledged the King's health and the health of Queen Mary at the end of the meal. This, though none of us could know it at the time, was the last great family gathering. For the next week or two the program was indeed a crowded one, with Court balls, ball suppers, drives round London, dinner parties, afternoon tea parties, and other entertainments. A feature of those days was that when large-scale entertainments were going on at Buckingham Palace the State drawing rooms were always perfumed with incense. This was in accordance with a rule of Queen Mary. She believed that incense burned like this kept away colds and other infections.

The King's health was again giving concern to his doctors, but Queen Mary, however worried she may have been inwardly, showed no sign that anything was wrong, and the preparations for rejoicings on the grand scale of those days went forward with zest. Some small idea of the kind of scale of Royal life then is to be found in the fact that every day the menus for the Royal table and the Household dining room were specially printed in an office at the Palace, not typed or cyclostyled. Those for the Royal table bore the joint cypher of the King and Queen in gold.

On Jubilee Day everything seemed perfect. The King, we learned later, was in more or less constant pain from his old operation, but no hint of this crept out. In all the Messes of the Palace there was open house all day, with lots to eat and drink for all on the staff, and for all the friends we had been allowed to bring in. Cold salmon, chickens, roast beef, delicious sweets, ice creams, fruits, champagne, whisky, port, and sherry —all were in plentiful supply at the King's orders, with no miserly counting of bottles or calculating portions. Lavish was the word for Royal hospitality in those days. Lavish, too, was the sprouting of new medals at the Palace that day. Everyone, men and women alike, above a certain station in the Household, and people who had been more than a certain number of years in the Royal service, in whatever capacity, were given the Jubilee Medal, with a ribbon of red, blue, and silver, and a silver medal showing the King and Queen in profile. It carried no letters after one's name, but everyone who received it was very proud of the King's gift.

After the great day was over we settled down to a more normal routine, and the King, enormously impressed by the wave of popular emotion which his Jubilee had produced, decided to make several drives round London, north, south, east, and west, at weekends, to show himself and the Queen to their subjects. It was something quite new in the way of Royal drives. Wherever they went they were acclaimed by hundreds of thousands of people. King George V, a man of great self-control, rarely showed emotion, but on each day when he had driven out among his subjects and heard their spontaneous greetings he came back to the Palace visibly moved. I am sure that the loyalty and affection that were shown him and Queen Mary in that month of May did much to make what was to be his last year on earth a happy one.

CHAPTER THREE

Three Royal Weddings

I HELPED to organize the catering side of three Royal weddings while I was at Buckingham Palace. The first was that of the lovely Princess Marina of Greece to the handsome young Prince George, Duke of Kent, who died so tragically eight years later in the wartime air crash in Scotland.

The Duke of Kent's wedding was the first to be celebrated in the Royal Family since the marriage of the Duke and Duchess of York, later King George VI and Queen Elizabeth, eleven years earlier. So when we came back to London from Balmoral in the autumn of 1934 there was a great deal of searching among dusty files for old menus, lists of those to be invited, and so on, by officials of the Lord Chamberlain's department and members of the Household staff charged with making the arrangements. The whole building was full of excitement and activity, from the high officials who saw the King and Queen each day, down to the humblest servants.

The young bridegroom, with his headquarters at York House, St. James's Palace, where he lived with his brother, the then Prince of Wales, made frequent visits to the Palace to consult officials, and to come to see us in my department about the catering arrangements. He was always rather shy and nervous, and the approach of his marriage seemed to have increased his shyness. He was constantly in and out of our

37

office worrying about every detail. His father, on the other hand, had a supreme and well-placed confidence in the ability of his staff to cope with any situation. Although the wedding was to be on November 1, the King left Buckingham Palace for Sandringham a fortnight before to spend ten days' shooting with a bachelor party. Queen Mary, who loved organizing big-scale functions, was left at Buckingham Palace in complete charge of the rest of the arrangements.

King George and Queen Mary were delighted at their youngest son's choice. I have sometimes thought since that King George V hoped that the example set by his youngest son would make his eldest, the Prince of Wales, take to the idea of marriage more kindly. Nothing would have given King George V greater pleasure, I am certain, than to see his beloved heir, David—as Edward, Prince of Wales, was always known in the Royal Family circle—settle down happily with a woman of his own choice of whom the family could approve.

We did not see anything of the Westminster Abbey ceremony, of course, but at Buckingham Palace on the wedding day all was bustle and excitement. I was amazed at the lavishness of the arrangements. The wedding breakfast was hospitality on the grand scale, nor did the mere question of how much it would cost the Privy Purse seem to matter at all when luncheon was served in the Steward's Room, the Officials' Mess, and the Servants' Hall, in each of which there were cold chicken and ham, with plentiful champagne, whisky, and port. When the wedding breakfast was over, the newly created Duke of Kent, with his Duchess, posed for the photographers before they left for their honeymoon. As they were driven away from the Palace in an open landau, the King, the Queen, and the other members of the Royal Family stood waiting in the forecourt to shower confetti, paper, and rose leaves on the newlyweds. It was a delightful family gathering, and a new insight for me into the ways of Royalty.

For the next two weeks, however, I did not perhaps take quite such a sympathetic view of Royal weddings. This one meant an enormous amount of work for us. Every day lists were sent down to me by Queen Mary with the names of people to whom she wished to send portions of the wedding cake. As for other Royal weddings, as I was to find out later, a number of huge wedding cakes were sent into Buckingham Palace by the leading cake and biscuit manufacturers.

The finest and largest of these was placed on a sideboard backed by a huge mirror in the Ball Supper Room—one of the State apartments on the first floor. It was in this room that the wedding breakfast for the Duke and Duchess of Kent was served. It is a magnificent apartment with a very large and heavy chandelier of gleaming crystal in the center of the ceiling, and large mirrors round all the walls. When it was ready for the wedding breakfast it was a delightful sight, with round-topped tables laid with spotless linen cloths, beautifully polished gold knives and forks and cruets, with roses and carnations in the center of each table. On sideboards around the room items from the magnificent collection of State Gold Plate were displayed under the soft lights of the candelabra, with mirrors reflecting them again and again, adding to the magnificence of it all.

The Kents' wedding cake, I remember, was five tiers in height, of lovely white icing. It was the most magnificent of all the Royal wedding cakes I have ever seen, except that for our present Queen, when she married in November, 1947. It took two Royal chefs all their time for five or six days to break up and cut into portions all the cakes that had been accepted for the Royal pair. Each portion was wrapped in greasepaper and put in a small parcel bearing in silver lettering the initials of the bride and bridegroom. Portions that were leftover were cut up and delivered by Royal motorcar to various hospitals, at the command of Queen Mary.

Fate decreed that the next Royal wedding should be on a much smaller scale. Only a short time before the King's third son, Prince Henry, Duke of Gloucester, was due to marry the lovely Lady Alice Montagu-Douglas-Scott, daughter of the Duke of Buccleuch, an old friend of the King's, the Duke was taken seriously ill and died. It was decided to cancel the ceremony at the Abbey and the big reception, and to hold the wedding in the private chapel at Buckingham Palace. So Prince Henry—Harry as he was known in the Royal circles— and his bride were married in complete privacy, with just the family and friends at the ceremony. Though the Duchess, small of figure, friendly of countenance, was deeply upset by the death of her father, she was a radiant bride, and I can remember now the lovely smile which she gave to all of us when she left the Palace with her tall, soldier husband.

The wedding of our present Queen was the first to take place from Buckingham Palace since the weddings of the Duke of Kent and the Duke of Gloucester, and again all sorts of records had to be consulted. But the changed conditions necessitated by the war and the shortages from which we were suffering in those days called for a great deal of replanning.

For instance, the wedding breakfast for Prince George, the Duke of Kent, and his bride consisted of ten courses. But when it came to arrange the wedding breakfast for Princess Elizabeth and Lieutenant Mountbatten, we were ordered by the King not to exceed the permitted three courses.

Some time before the wedding a number of cakes had arrived at Buckingham Palace. Every cake manufacturer connected with the Royal Family, or holding a Royal Warrant of Appointment, was allowed, by the King's orders, to give a cake for the wedding of the Princess. Nine cakes in all had arrived at the Palace, and I arranged for them to be placed on a long trestle table in the middle of the State Dining Room, the highest cake in the center, and the smaller ones tapering away to the left and right. Around the walls of the State Dining Room are large mirrors, and each of these, reflecting the nine cakes, made the impression of whiteness all the greater.

The King and Queen arranged that all the directors of the cake- and biscuit-making firms who had presented the gift of cakes should come to Buckingham Palace. They came from Edinburgh, Manchester, Liverpool, Reading as well as from London, and they were summoned to be present at the Palace at a certain time one afternoon so that they could be presented to the King and Queen and give Their Majesties details of the ingredients of the cakes and the various recipes from which they were made, and explain the designs, including the various coats of arms which adorned the icing. Their appointed time for arrival at Buckingham Palace was at half-past two. By twenty-five to three eight of them had arrived, but the ninth was nowhere to be found. Telephone calls to the hotel where he was staying were of no avail. Eventually the Master of the Household decided that the King and Queen could not be kept waiting and the eight directors who had arrived must be shown up to the State Dining Room.

Still there was no sign of the missing director. I went several times downstairs and searched the Palace to make sure that he had not got lost (as had happened before to new visitors) in the main corridors leading from the Tradesmen's Entrance up to the State Apartments. But there was no sign of him anywhere. His eight rivals spent a happy hour talking to the King and Queen and receiving Their Majesties' congratulations. It was two or three hours later that the door of my office opened and the missing director came bustling in in a highly nervous state. He told me how terribly sorry he was, but he was late because of trouble with his car on his way to London. He quite understood that he had missed his chance of talking to the King and Queen, but he implored me, almost with tears in his eyes, to allow him to go up and see his firm's cake on view with those of his rivals. Feeling sorry for him, I readily consented, and led him up the back stairs to the State Dining Room. Then I left him and went ahead. Opening the door, I was surprised to find the King and Queen still in the room, engaged in looking at all the cakes and examining their decorations in detail.

I stepped forward and explained to the Queen why I was there and why I had brought my visitor up to see his own cake. Then Queen Elizabeth, with that friendly sympathy for others that is such a great characteristic of hers, smiled and said to me, "Bring him in by all means." I went outside, and without telling the director what was going on, beckoned him into the room. He was indeed surprised when he found the King and Queen standing there, smiling, waiting to shake him by the hand. For twenty minutes he was alone with them, and had a much longer talk than any of his rivals.

The Royal wedding day was one of large-scale festivities at Buckingham Palace, even though there was not such lavish entertainment as at the wedding of the Duke of Kent. But there was champagne for everyone, and rarely has a toast to a Royal bride been drunk with more enthusiasm than that which we in the various messes at the Palace drank on that day of November 20, 1947, to our beloved Princess Elizabeth, now our Queen. I was delighted later when the Princess sent a personal message to all of us on the Household staff who had helped in the arrangements for her wedding, saying how satisfied and delighted she was with everything that had been done. But my connection with the wedding was by no means over. I was ordered by the King to go to Balmoral to prepare Birkhall, the small house near the Castle, for the reception of the Princess and her husband, who were going to spend the second part of their honeymoon there. After two days making these preparations I came back to London, leaving Birkhall in possession of the newlyweds.

Back at the Palace there was the same routine of cutting the wedding cakes into small pieces for distribution to the Princess's personal friends. Several thousand pieces of cake were dispatched from Buckingham Palace, each in a small white cardboard box with the Royal initials, "EP," on the lid in silver. Again the remainder of the cakes were cut into large slices and distributed among the various hospitals at the Princess's orders. She also gave orders for pieces of her cakes to be sent to various regiments with which she had personal connections. On the night of the Royal wedding, after the bride and bridegroom had left Buckingham Palace, there was a small dinner party given by the King and Queen. It was an intimate little occasion tinged with sadness at the absence of their daughter. But, like his father before him at his own marriage, and at that of the Duke of Gloucester, the King was delighted beyond measure that his elder daughter had found her married happiness with a man of her choice so eminently suitable as the Duke of Edinburgh.

CHAPTER FOUR

Catering for Celebrations

WITH memories of the Coronation of Queen Elizabeth II so recent in our minds, it is difficult to recall the splendors of the Coronation of her father. Although the Monarchy was at that time severely shaken by the abdication of the much-beloved King Edward VIII, in the short period of not quite six months between King George VI's accession in December, 1936, and his Coronation on May 6, 1937, he had, with the aid, comfort, and support of his Queen, already won millions of hearts throughout the Commonwealth, and there was enormous rejoicing as Coronation Day approached.

At Buckingham Palace there was the usual hustle and bustle caused by preparations for a great event. This time everything was made much more complicated by the fact that provisional plans had been worked out many months before for the Coronation of a bachelor King. Even the draft program of the Abbey processions had been prepared. When the new King and his Queen came to the throne all these plans had to be abandoned and others made by the Earl Marshal, the Duke of Norfolk. This was the young Duke's first experience of a Coronation, and I must say that in our view he acquitted himself very well indeed. We saw a good deal of him at Buckingham Palace, and though he looked quite harassed and worried by the weight of his responsibilities, he usually managed to find the answers to the problems involved. If he could not solve the problems himself he never had any hesitation in going to the older members of the Court, whose memories went back to the Coronation of King George V, and asking them about various details.

It was twenty-six years since the last Coronation, and though in its essential features the Coronation has scarcely changed for centuries, various details of the ceremonial are altered with each Sovereign. To us in the Supply Office the Coronation meant many weeks of real hard work. We had to organize every item of the supplies for the State Banquet on the Coronation Eve, for the luncheon which was to follow the Coronation ceremony, at which we were told to prepare for at least four hundred guests, and many other functions.

One of the biggest problems, I remember, which was repeated again at the Coronation of Queen Elizabeth II, was providing food for the King and Queen and the great Officers of State who would be in attendance on them at Westminster Abbey itself. While people outside in the Mall were lying sleeping, wrapped in topcoats, ground-sheets, and blankets in the rain of the very early morning hours, we inside the Palace, who had been up until past midnight dealing with the preparation of the State banquet at which the King and Queen had entertained their Royal guests, were up again before four o'clock.

The first duty we had was to arrange for the refreshments to be taken over to the Abbey. They had to leave in an Army lorry by 4:30 A.M., so as to comply with the police regulation to keep the streets clear after that hour for Coronation movements. It was no very elaborate menu that was sent over to the Abbey for the refreshment of the newly crowned King and Queen. There were mutton pies, stuffed rolls, sweet biscuits—all made and prepared in the Royal kitchens—with some cold chicken and cold ham. There was also, of course, champagne, whisky, and port, sent over from the Royal cellars. All the necessary plant—glasses, plates, knives, forks, spoons, and napkins—also had to be sent across from Buckingham Palace, counted carefully when they were taken out, and checked when they were brought back, for souvenir hunters are not unknown, even in places like Westminster Abbey.

Throughout Coronation Day, 1937, the Palace was an open house. There was a champagne lunch for every member of the staff at the Palace, with the guests that he or she had wished to bring in to see the procession from the forecourt. All the workers from the estates at Balmoral, Sandringham, and Windsor had been invited by the King and Queen to the Palace for the day. I do not ever remember seeing Buckingham Palace so crowded as on that lovely May day, and everyone was happy and gay. But some of us could not help thinking of the man who might have been the central figure of all those rejoicings—the Duke of Windsor, now overseas, unwanted and almost forgotten.

It was four o'clock in the afternoon before the newly crowned King and Queen got back to the Palace. Both of them looked quite fresh and radiant in their Coronation robes and still wearing their crowns. But the Queen told her personal maid that she was very tired and had a headache from the weight of her crown.

I remember seeing the newly crowned King and Queen at very close quarters indeed. As I stood in the corridor on the first floor with my mother and my wife, they passed along to go out onto the balcony to make their first appearance before the crowds outside. Following them came the tall, regal figure of Queen Mary, and then the two Princesses, Elizabeth and Margaret, each wearing a golden coronet of their rank, with a charming simply cut Coronation dress. The Dukes of

Kent and Gloucester with their Duchesses, all in their Royal robes of gold and red, and wearing coronets, followed behind. It was indeed an impressive glimpse of the Royal Family, and one I shall never forget. That evening a simple three-course dinner was served to the King and Queen, who ate alone. They were emotionally much moved by the experiences they had gone through and very tired. Then followed crowded weeks of a heavy program of engagements which took the King and Queen to Windsor Castle for Ascot, to Spithead for the Naval Review, to the Palace of Holyroodhouse for a State visit to Scotland, and to many other places all over the country.

Another great day of celebration and rejoicing at Buckingham Palace of a rather different kind was VE-Day. All day long there were great crowds outside the Palace gates, cheering and calling for the King and Queen. For some days it had been obvious that the war was at its end in Europe, after the British and American and Russian armies, with their French allies, had entered Berlin. Now the news was official. That afternoon arrangements had been made for the King to be photographed with members of his victorious War Cabinet on the Bow Room steps in the garden. Because the crowds along the front of Buckingham Palace and in the Mall were so huge that the police were quite unable to move them to clear a way for the arrival of the various Ministers, it was decided that they should come into the Palace by that secret side door in Buckingham Palace Road known as the Electricians' Gate. Accordingly, the police made Herculean efforts and cleared the way so that the Prime Minister's car, followed by those of his Cabinet colleagues, could enter the Palace from Buckingham Palace Road. To enter by the front gates was absolutely impossible.

I have never heard such cheers as those which greeted Mr.

Churchill as his car, moving at a snail's pace, approached the front of the Palace and turned to pass the Trade Gate. The great wartime Prime Minister was standing in the back of the open car with his hand extended in the famous V-sign. He was bareheaded, with a large cigar in his mouth, and a happy smile of victory on his face. Next came Mr. Attlee, who also received great cheers from the crowd. There were cheers, too, for the other members of the Cabinet as the crowd recognized them one by one. All so far had gone well. But the chauffeur driving the late Mr. Ernest Bevin, the Foreign Secretary, had been caught up in the huge crowds which by now had spread all over the road, bursting through the police barriers. Despite every effort by the police, no way could be cleared for the Foreign Secretary's car. So the chauffeur, finding himself unable to proceed to the Electricians' Gate, was guided by the police to the nearest gate, the Tradesmen's Entrance.

Mr. Bevin was most upset as his car came to a standstill just outside the Palace Police lodge. When he was asked to get out of his car in the yard, the Foreign Secretary was most indignant. It was suggested that he should allow himself to be escorted the few yards into the garden by a door in the wall which is situated just behind the Royal kitchen. Then the Foreign Secretary put his foot down. "No, I won't," he declared. "I'm not getting out at any tradesmen's entrance," he said to the Palace policeman. So the police, almost fighting with the crowds, struggled to make a way for his car, which backed out into the roadway and went slowly on to the Electricians' Gate. He was the last to arrive to complete the group, and there was a lot of leg-pulling, led by the King, about the Foreign Secretary nearly missing this historic picture.

That night the King gave a little dinner party in the Palace for members of his family. After dinner he and the Queen made many balcony appearances, with Princess Elizabeth, in the khaki uniform of an officer in the Auxiliary Transport Service, and Princess Margaret at their sides. It was well after midnight before lights in the Royal apartments were turned out. As a sequel to V-E Day the King and Queen gave a series of afternoon parties for the various Services, including the Civil Defense Corps and the Women's Land Army.

Gradually, as the weeks passed, Buckingham Palace began to take on a more normal appearance. The windows which had been blown out on the front of the Palace, and had been replaced temporarily by horrid stuff that looked like white muslin, were reglazed. The chandeliers were rehung in the State Rooms and a general tidying-up began which took many months to complete. Rooms that had been closed for six long years were reopened, cleaned, and made ready for use as members of the Royal Household and of the Household staff gradually began to filter back from their wartime service. Soon the King put aside his uniform and appeared as we used to know him before the war, in well-cut lounge suits of the quiet grays and blues which he specially favored. That seemed to us in the Palace to be the most definite and convincing sign that the war was indeed over.

In the days of King George V, when I first went to Buckingham Palace, the whole of Royal life seemed to me, as I looked at it with fresh eyes, to be one long round of State ceremonies. This indeed was partly true, for in those days the whole life of the King was much more filled with ceremonies of various kinds than is the case today. King George V always enjoyed the calm, orderly ritual of great State occasions and was a magnificent figure at the center of them.

CHAPTER FIVE

Racing at Cowes and Ascot

Two of the most impressive periods of the year in those days were Ascot Week at Windsor Castle, and the fortnight at Cowes, when the King and Queen lived aboard their yacht, the *Victoria and Albert,* and the King went racing every day in his beloved sailing yacht, the *Britannia.* The whole of Cowes Fortnight was one procession of entertainments of the most lavish and exclusive kind. Every little detail was thought out in advance. These were the two weeks of the year which the King enjoyed, I think, more than any other. The same was not true of Queen Mary. Never a good sailor, she resolutely refused to accompany her husband aboard his racing yacht. Instead she would go ashore to the Isle of Wight from the *Victoria and Albert,* and spend her afternoons looking at antique shops or touring the beauty spots of the island.

Accommodation aboard the *Victoria and Albert* was very limited and not very comfortable, so there was no keen competition among members of the Royal staff to go down to Cowes. The minimum number of servants would be taken and everyone had to do about two men's work. But even so a large number of servants went down in advance to Portsmouth —two or three valets for the King, two dressers for the Queen, footmen and pages, with servants, valets, and ladies' maids for the gentlemen and ladies in attendance on Their Majesties, as well as two chefs, a roasting cook, and his assistant, two pastry cooks, and several others from the kitchens. Every evening, after the day's racing, the King would give a big dinner party on board his yacht. Nearly always the evening would be rounded off, in naval style, by the officers and ship's company of the Royal yacht giving a concert for the King and Queen. I often saw Queen Mary looking as though she could have found some more interesting way of passing her evening. But King George, with his love of Navy life, enjoyed every minute of these concerts, reveling in the simple humor of his sailors.

Supplies for the Royal yacht were largely purchased locally in Portsmouth, but a great many things had to come down from London. The best dessert fruit, and flowers, were sent daily to the harbor from the Royal gardens at Windsor and were brought over from Portsmouth in one of the *Victoria and Albert's* barges. So, too, were the King's specially made cream cheeses, which came from the Royal dairy at Windsor. One member of the staff (I did the job myself many times) had the duty of going over to Portsmouth to meet the express from Waterloo and take from the guard the packet addressed to, "H. M. THE KING, Royal Yacht, Cowes." Another item to which much importance was attached was the crescent rolls which the King always ate at luncheon and dinner. These were made, not at Buckingham Palace, but in the bakery of a well-known London catering firm. They were sent down to Portsmouth every day on the early morning train.

So important were these rolls that they, like the cream cheeses, were placed in the personal charge of the guard on the train, who had instructions to deliver them to a member of the catering firm's staff who would meet the train at Portsmouth. This particular member of the firm always spent the fortnight at Cowes dressed in a blue yachting suit and a

51

jaunty yachting cap. Once he had picked up the box of rolls he boarded a naval pinnace to be taken over to the Royal yacht. That was all he had to do, and his firm, in those days, thought it worth while to pay his expenses for the fortnight just to ensure that the King of England received his rolls safely. Nothing like that happens today.

The Cowes Fortnight is still a great social event, but it is not what it was in the more spacious days. Though the interest in yachting is maintained, and the Duke of Edinburgh encourages lovers of the sport by his own devotion to yachting, things are emphatically not the same.

Ascot, on the other hand, remains very nearly what it was in earlier days, but even at the Royal meetings things are not quite the same as when I first went to the Palace. I shall never forget the first time I saw the Royal table being laid for dinner in the beautiful State Dining Room at Windsor Castle, where King George V and Queen Mary always entertained a large party. This magnificent room is flanked on either side by the beautiful Crimson Drawing Room and a room known as the Octagon Room. The State Dining Room has a wonderful outlook over the lovely Royal golf course and across country to Staines and Egham. Great chandeliers of shining crystal light the room. When all is ready for dinner it is a magnificent sight to behold, with the long table exquisitely laid for at least thirty and sometimes over forty people. Beautifully shaped gold and silver vases from the Royal collection filled with sweet peas, carnations, and roses from the Royal gardens stand on the long table between the gold forks, spoons, cruets, and glasses. On the walls of the room are the heavy pieces of priceless gold plate. It takes the underbutlers two hours or more to complete the laying of the table, even in these simpler days.

Dessert was always a great feature of the Royal menus in the days of King George V. Figs, plums, apples, pears, and grapes from the Royal hothouses were placed along the table in lovely china dishes of various ware, just before the King and Queen led their guests into the room.

A military string band provided by the Guards always play a selection of light music at the Royal dinner parties at Windsor Castle in Ascot Week. They are stationed in the Minstrels' Gallery—some thirty musicians under a Director of Music. The bandsmen are provided with beer and sandwiches in the servants' hall, while the Director is always given a large whisky and soda and a sandwich when the performance is over.

In those days it was the rule that the King and Queen and their guests took lunch in the Royal Stand at Ascot. Every day the elaborate Royal lunch was sent over to the course from the kitchens at Windsor Castle, with chefs and servants to wait on the Royal Family and their guests. At 12:15 exactly, the King, in a frockcoat, with his trousers pressed in the individual fashion that he maintained throughout his life, at the sides instead of at the front, would come out of the Sovereign's Entrance into the quadrangle. Already the four Royal Princes, with the Castle guests, would be gathered in the quadrangle awaiting the King's arrival.

The King and Queen would enter the leading car, followed by other members of the Royal Family and their guests, then the long procession of cars would pull slowly away from the Castle and proceed majestically along the Long Walk in Windsor Great Park toward Ascot. At the Golden Gate by the racecourse the Royal party would dismount and enter the open landaus drawn by gray horses with postilions in Ascot State (which means a special livery of red and gold and blue, the Royal racing colors) to drive onto the course and round it into the Entrance to the Royal Enclosure and so to the Royal Box.

Today almost exactly the same procedure is observed by Queen Elizabeth II and her husband, the Duke of Edinburgh, every year except in 1955, when the railway strike caused the meeting to be postponed, and robbed it of half its Royal glory. Queen Elizabeth II has inherited much of her grandfather's love of exact timing and punctuality, and the Royal drives from Windsor to Ascot are planned with just as much precision as they were in his days.

One of the great features of Ascot Week under King George V, which was suspended during the years after the war but has now been revived, was the famous strawberry-and-cream teas. It was usually five o'clock when the Royal party got back from the races. Tea was served at once in the Orangery of the Castle for some sixty or seventy people. Luscious strawberries, specially cultivated by the Royal gardeners under glass, were served with cream from the Royal dairies. There was gay talk of the day's racing for an hour or more, then the King and Queen and their guests left for their rooms to change for dinner. Today much the same procedure is observed, but as well as strawberries and cream, cocktails and sherry usually are served. Another change nowadays is that luncheon is no longer served in the Royal Box at Ascot, the Queen and her guests taking instead a simple luncheon at the Castle before going to the races. The Ascot Week is one which the present Queen enjoys as much as any of the weeks of her year. Racing is really one of her great interests, in which she takes after her great-grandfather, certainly not after her father or grandfather, for neither King George V nor King George VI had any keen personal interest in racing.

54

The one feature of Ascot that has remained unchanged from the days of King George V until today is the complete ban on divorced people in the Royal Enclosure. Even the influence of the war years, with the breaking-down of the old standards, left this Royal rule unchanged. King George VI, approached many times by many different people, would hear nothing of any change in the regulations. Yet to many of us in the Royal service it was a well-known fact that some "borderline" cases were admitted to the Royal Enclosure every year, with or without the King's knowledge. And knowing as we did how much the King made himself acquainted with all that was going on among people he knew, we could not believe that he was unaware of these cases.

I am not suggesting for a moment that anyone got into the Royal Enclosure under false pretenses. The system of checking and counter-checking at the Ascot office run under the control of the Duke of Norfolk, Her Majesty's Representative at Ascot, is too fine for that to happen. But there were people in society, titled ones among them, whom we well knew had been involved in divorce cases, even if their names had not been mentioned in court. These were admitted without question to the Royal Enclosure, and it always seemed to me that the rule was not so much, "do not become involved in a divorce case," as "if you must become involved in a divorce case, take great care not to get your name into the papers or to be named in court."

Queen Elizabeth has now solved the problem in a way of her own by making for the first time at Ascot a new sort of Royal Enclosure, which, though it still bears one name, is not quite so exclusive. Here the no-divorce rule is not so rigidly applied. The Queen and members of her own party from Windsor Castle, of course, have their own enclosure within the enclosure, known as the Queen's Lawn, and here the rules

55

are as rigid as ever. It is only fair, however, to the memory of King George VI to say that some plan of this kind had been laid before him without his disapproval in the last year or so of his life, when the big improvements in the stands and enclosures at Ascot were originally planned.

CHAPTER SIX

How Buckingham Palace Works

Buckingham Palace, home of the world's most powerful remaining monarchy, is, to those who look at it from the outside, a place of mystery and romance, a kind of fairy-tale building where almost anything may happen. To those of us who have worked inside the Palace, of course, things seem very different. In fact Buckingham Palace is run partly as a big business concern and partly as a big hotel. In my own department—that of the Comptroller of Supply—naturally I was mostly concerned with the hotel side of the Palace. Kings and Queens, their immediate suites, their officials, and their servants, all have to be fed just like ordinary mortals. So one of the essential parts of the Royal service is to provide enough food of the right kind for all the different people who are eating within the Palace precincts. It is a little-known fact that part of the perquisites of members of the Royal Household is the liberty to come to Buckingham Palace to eat any meal—breakfast, lunch, tea, or dinner—any day when the court is in residence, whether the person who wants to come and eat is actually on duty or not.

The essential of all good hotels is that they shall run smoothly and perfectly and that the customers shall always be satisfied. These considerations apply equally to Buckingham Palace, even more so, perhaps, than to any hotel, for the "clients" consist first of all of the Sovereign and his or her Consort, and then the people immediately in attendance upon them, all of them high dignitaries of State accustomed always to the most perfect service.

It was part of my job to see that in one direction at least they got it. I am proud to think that in all the years I was at Buckingham Palace there were few if any complaints from the King or Queen, or any members of the Royal Family, about the quality of the food that was put before them. In the war, of course, as I shall explain more fully later, it was indeed difficult to keep up the high standard demanded, and many were the subterfuges to which we had to resort to keep up even the semblance of a prewar standard. But King George VI and Queen Elizabeth were most understanding people. They never complained, even when things were not quite what they should have been. It seemed to me, whenever I spoke to the King or Queen, that they understood, as many of the officials of the Royal Household did not always seem to understand, just exactly what the difficulties were that faced me in my constant efforts to provide what was wanted.

All food and all drink supplied to Buckingham Palace, whether for the personal consumption of the King and Queen or for consumption by other members of their staff, come from tradesmen who hold the Royal Warrant of Appointment. There is a lot of misunderstanding about this question of holding the Royal Warrant. In the days of George V the regulations had become rather slack, and there were a very considerable number of tradesmen who held, legitimately, Warrants of Appointment, but who in fact rarely supplied very much to Buckingham Palace. One of the first things that King George VI did when he came to the throne was to send for a complete list of all the tradespeople who had supplied his father. He sat down to revise and reduce this list drastically.

With his high notions of the importance of the Royal Family, King George VI was determined right from the beginning of his reign that not even in the smallest and least important particular should there be any doubt whatever about the honors connected with Buckingham Palace. He introduced, for example, the rule, which is still current today, that if you hold the Royal Warrant of Appointment you must put on your notepaper and the labels on your product exactly what it is that you hold the warrant for. For example, if a firm of provision merchants supplies, say, only the pickles for the Royal table, they must put the words, "By appointment to His [or Her] Majesty—Purveyors of Pickles," so as to make it clear that they do not supply the Royal Family with any of their other products.

King George VI also reintroduced an old rule that Royal tradesmen must have supplied the Palace with goods for at least three years to the complete satisfaction of Their Majesties and the Master of the Household and the Lord Chamberlain, who are the two high officials responsible for Royal Warrants, except in the case of warrants dealing with horses and saddlery, which come under the Crown Equerry and the Master of the Horse.

When the third anniversary of the accession of Queen Elizabeth II passed without any Warrants of Appointment being given, some people wondered whether the Queen had decided to alter the rules governing warrants. She had not. All that happened was that the Queen decided that she would, as her father had done before her, examine the claims of every single Royal tradesman in person before allowing the warrants to go out. This, interspersed among her many State duties, meant some considerable delay, and it was not until several months later that the warrants were ready for handing out, and that the new Royal tradesmen could proudly display outside their shops the Queen's Arms. Incidentally, it is not only among the big shops in the West End and the famous ones in St. James's Street and elsewhere, that you will find the Royal Warrants. There are shops in Glasgow, in Edinburgh, in King's Lynn, and in Windsor, which also display the Royal Arms.

During the war, when many things were in short supply, there were not wanting tradesmen with an eye to the main chance and the future, who attempted to win Royal favor by sending in goods of various kinds which were difficult to obtain, in the hope that we, in the Comptroller of Supply Department, would give them a recommendation so that eventually they, too, could become proud possessors of the Royal Warrant. Unfortunately for these people, their plan was too obvious, and it was only from firms we knew and could trust that either my chief, Mr. James Kennedy, or I ever would accept articles in short supply, however urgent the demand or need for them was.

Food—that subject of interest to everyone, King or commoner—was the main part of my job at the Palace throughout the years, so I came to have a firsthand, intimate knowledge of most of the likes and dislikes of members of the Royal Family.

In the old days, Kings, with all the resources of unlimited purses behind them, often were leaders in the gastronomic arts, vying with one another, and with the great nobles of their own countries, in the creation of new, exotic dishes which would carry their names down to posterity, so that today many world-renowned dishes are called after Kings of long ago, their favorites, and their chefs. I am bound to report that, even in the most lavish days I knew at the Palace, in the reign of George V, no such ambition stirred in the breast of any member of our Royal Family. Generally speaking, their tastes have been, and are, for the ordinary simple foods, plainly cooked without fancy trimmings, and with only one imperative condition applying to everything served at the Royal table: it must be of the very first quality.

It is a Royal tradition that at wedding breakfasts and State banquets, the King's Chef evolves one or two dishes which he names to commemorate the occasion, but these are nearly always just variants on old recipes, and none have merited a special place in the cookery books. Neither our present Queen nor her father could be counted among the gastronomic experts, and these special dishes were regarded by King George VI without any favor. He would much have preferred a plain dish of his own choosing, and would sigh with relief when, at the end of a State visit, he could return to the menus of good, simple English food that pleased him most.

The question of exactly how the Royal Family get their food each day is one that seems to interest many people. It is all quite simple, and again the system used corresponds very largely with that in operation at any of the famous hotels. Everyday items, like bread, meat, fish, poultry, are ordered by telephone. These orders originate with the Royal Chef, who sends requisitions in to my own old department, that of the Comptroller of Supply, whose responsibility it is to see that there is always enough of everything in the Palace larders and storerooms to meet every need, not only of the Royal Family, but also of the couple of hundred men and women of the Household and staff who eat at the Palace every day.

Members of the Royal Family do not see these goods at all until they reach the table, any more than anyone staying at the Ritz or Claridge's would expect to see the food delivered to the hotel kitchens. The Royal food deliveries are made to the Trade Door in Buckingham Palace Road, and taken direct to the kitchens, where a storeman receives them, noting each item in a ledger, which used to be handed to me each month for stocktaking. The kitchens and storerooms at the Palace are on a really Royal scale. There is enough room in the big refrigerator, for example, to keep literally hundreds of chickens or game birds, and scores of pounds of meat. This cold store—there is as yet no deep freeze at the Palace—is some 8 ft. 6 in. high and over 15 ft. square. In normal peacetime it is a sight to see, filled with fine capons from the Royal farms, grouse, pheasant, and partridge, lobsters, salmon, prime meat, and similar items. It is kept locked night and day, with duplicate keys in possession of the Chef himself and the chief storeman. Whatever the Chef wants for the preparation of the day's menus, he writes out on a chit, which the storekeeper later hands into my office to be entered in the ledgers, so that a constant check is kept on every item of food used, every ounce of butter, every egg from the Royal farms, again just as in a big hotel, thus ensuring both efficiency and economy.

The King's Chef has an office, complete with desk and telephone, on the ground floor near his kitchens. (I recall that in the days of the last French chef, M. Roussin, it was difficult to enter that office, because of the strong and pervading smell of garlic, of which he was inordinately fond!) Here, each afternoon when lunch is over, the Chef sits down to compose a carefully balanced menu for the Royal lunch and dinner the following day. This he writes out in the Royal menu book, which later goes up to the Queen for her approval. Though far from a gourmet, the Queen has decided views about food, and gives the menu suggestions her closest attention, frequently crossing out some item and writing in a substitute of her own choice. We were always prepared for such Royal preferences, and in the reserve stock of foodstuffs nearly always there were whatever ingredients were needed to make the dishes the Queen wanted. If by chance something was missing, a little telephoning, and a taxi ride by one of the Palace messengers or orderlies, would soon procure what was wanted. In the whole of my time at the Palace, apart from the war years of shortages, I cannot remember one single instance of a Royal wish going unfulfilled in the matter of food.

A Royal lunch menu for six to eight people usually consists of an hors d'œuvres (these were never featured on the Palace menu until the advent of the Duke of Edinburgh, who has a special fondness for them), or an egg dish, followed by roast neck of lamb, or a grill, with the appropriate vegetables (always those in season, eaten fresh from the Royal gardens at Windsor), followed by a light sweet, such as a *crêpe suzette, a millefeuille aux pommes,* or a compote of fruit with cream. Very rarely indeed are more than three courses served.

For dinner, a typical menu would be consommé, followed by a fillet of sole, halibut, or turbot, a roast such as partridge, chicken, or pheasant, again with appropriate vegetables (the Queen is particularly fond of what the French call *primeurs*— baby carrots, new peas, very young spinach, and tiny new potatoes), with a sweet such as a *crème caramel,* a *bavarois à la vanille,* a *tarte aux cerises, framboises,* or *fraises* (the French names are still retained on the Royal menus), followed by a savory like *croûtes de merluche* (Scotch woodcock) with coffee and dessert. Fruit is always on the Royal table throughout the year, nectarines, apples, pears, plums, grapes, peaches, tangerines, oranges, and green figs, each in its season.

It is significant of the tastes of the late King and Her present Majesty that the head of the kitchen at Buckingham Palace today is a tall, dark-haired, clean-shaven, cheerful Yorkshireman, called Ronald Aubrey. He was chosen by King George VI as the first English chef to be appointed at the Palace for many years. Previously Frenchmen had reigned supreme. King George, I remember, before the war, decided as a matter of policy to introduce English cooking to the Palace, not only for his own table, but for official lunches and dinners as well, and it was with this end in view that Aubrey was given the job. The war interrupted the scheme, and the King's plan had to be shelved, while the Royal Chef left the spacious—though then very old-fashioned—kitchens of Buckingham Palace for the rough-and-ready environment of an R.A.F. mess. When he came back, of course, the Palace was still restricted by rationing, and it was not until the beginning of Queen Elizabeth II's reign that things got back to normal and Aubrey, with the consent of his Royal mistress, could introduce the full English menus he had planned for so long.

While the Queen was on her Commonwealth tour in 1954, she sent Aubrey to Paris to study at one of the big hotels, so that he could be fully prepared to produce any continental dishes which she might want for entertaining. Like other people, the Queen has her own particular likes and dislikes in food. For instance, with the finest grouse in the country readily available to her from the Balmoral moors, she dislikes that particular game bird, and roast grouse is never served to her. If grouse is the main item on a Royal menu—and the Queen does not allow her individual tastes to rob others of the pleasure of eating grouse—a separate dish, usually roast partridge, is served to the Queen.

All the Royal Family are abstemious people and drink very sparingly with their meals. For luncheon, usually mineral spring water is taken, though sherry, gin, vermouth, and whisky are on the sideboard beforehand, and there is always a supply of white and red wine and champagne brought up for lunch and dinner from the Royal cellars. This, too, is checked in and out, so that an exact account of the bottles used may be kept, which reminds me of an incident at Windsor Castle during the war days, where the quite proper and justifiable zeal of a Royal official led to some grumbling among certain servants, who imagined they were being done out of their "rights" (a favorite grouse among Royal servants) whereas in fact they were merely being brought back to the straight and narrow path.

It was in the billiard room at the Castle one night that Sir Piers Legh, the Master of the Household, playing with another member of the King's entourage, decided they should have a whisky apiece at the end of the game. But there was no whisky to be found in the billiard room. The decanters were empty. "Joey" Legh could not recall that any had been drunk since he last saw the decanters half-full or more, and summoned a footman to explain. No explanation was forthcoming, but Sir Piers guessed the answer with no difficulty. Next day he ordered me to procure an old-fashioned tantalus stand for the Castle billiard room, one of those affairs in which two decanters stand side by side, but neither can be opened until a bar across the top has been unlocked. From that day on the servants of the Castle, who had been in the habit of warming themselves with a good tot as they passed through the billiard room on their way to bed after a spell of Air Raid Protection or fire-watching duty, had to go without. Sir Piers' name was "mud," but the whisky consumption figures at the Castle diminished quite considerably.

From the savings' point of view, this was a good thing. But it was another example of the "new style" in the treatment of servants, who in the old days had regarded an occasional drink "on the house" as a recognized part of their wages. Nearly all such privileges have been wiped out nowadays, which may partly account for the difficulty of obtaining, and certainly of keeping, servants even in the Royal Household.

One or two examples of Royal tastes in foodstuffs come to mind as I look back. Queen Elizabeth, the Queen Mother, has a fondness for cold roast beef, done very rare. The Duke of Edinburgh likes oysters. The Queen cannot bear them. King George VI was as fond of dressed crab as of the potted shrimps I shall mention later. The Duke of Edinburgh, unlike most naval officers, does not care for pink gin. Queen Elizabeth prefers a small gin and orange to any other kind of *apéritif.* King George VI always drank his whisky with Malvern spring water, never neat or with soda, and did not care for champagne or heavy red wines. Another of Queen Elizabeth's great likings is for all kinds of shellfish, specially lobster. At Windsor Castle or Royal Lodge at weekends, a special lobster cocktail made to a recipe in the Queen Mother's own possession is a regular feature at the beginning of lunch on Sunday.

In wartime it was not always possible to obtain the necessary ingredients, especially the Tabasco sauce which is an essential item of the cocktail mixture. At the same time, by a curious coincidence, the stock of special Negri toothpicks which King George VI always used after every meal also came to an end. When the King was told of the shortage of his favorite toothpicks, he smiled, shrugged his shoulders, and said, "Oh, well, it's a very minor hardship in these days." The Queen, when she was told that there was no more Tabasco sauce, took the news philosophically. But neither of these things was a rationed commodity, and I had many friends among the West End tradesmen and caterers. So it was a minor triumph for me the following week when I was able to send a message to the King that a consignment of ten thousand toothpicks (enough, as it only too sadly turned out, to last him for the rest of his days) had arrived. I was also able to send a message to the Queen that enough bottles of Tabasco sauce had arrived to last for years, as only a few drops of it are used in making the lobster cocktail.

Throughout the war no one in the country conformed more strictly to the rationing laws than the King and Queen and Queen Mary. I was in a unique position to know this, since all the ordering and obtaining of foodstuffs for them passed through my hands. Of course, when official guests were to be entertained, extra rations were applied for and readily obtained from the local food offices at Westminster, King's Lynn, Windsor, or Aberdeen. But extra rations so obtained never went improperly to the King or Queen. Yet throughout all those difficult days I never once heard a complaint from any member of the Royal Family (though I am afraid I cannot say the same for members of the Royal Household and the staff).

Food from Sandringham, Windsor, and Balmoral was used extensively throughout the war to supplement the ordinary rations. Salmon from the Dee was an especially useful item. In the season, beginning in May, we would have two or three fine fish sent down every week, each weighing from eight and a half pounds to as much as sixteen pounds. This sufficed for grilled salmon steak on the Royal menu three or four times a week. When it was more plentiful in June and July with five or six fish arriving every week, the Queen gave orders for it to be served at the Royal breakfast table as a kedgeree, and also to be used up on the staff menu, privately rationed at three ounces per person.

There was one difficulty about the salmon, however, and that quite a major one. King George VI was not at all fond of it. So whenever it was on the menu another dish had to be cooked for him. One of his favorite alternatives was a well-trimmed lean lamb cutlet, but this, even for the King of England, was a rare luxury during the war, and the substitute dish for the salmon was usually another fish. The King preferred a fried fillet of sole, poached turbot or halibut, or, when they were obtainable, whiting. He liked a good sauce with his fish. He was never a big eater, but had his own definite ideas about what he wanted served to him. Time and again I would receive a direct request from him which had to be treated as a Royal command. Once at Balmoral his Page came into my office and said, "The King wants to know why he cannot have bacon like that served to him on the Royal train."

I did not travel on that train with the King, but had arrived in Scotland in advance, so I knew nothing about the Royal breakfast bacon. Hurried inquiries by telephone to the railway executives who had accompanied the King elicited the fact that the King had been served with egg and bacon for this breakfast, and that the bacon was ordinary streaky. This was difficult to understand, as I always made a point of buying a special piece of streaky bacon each week for the King's ration to be served for his breakfast. So I made some more inquiries, this time from the train chef. He told me that the bacon had been quick-fried and served rather underdone, whereas our own Chef sent the bacon to the King crisp and well fried. Thenceforth the King's streaky rashers were always served rather underdone.

Another breakfast taste which the King acquired on his train travels was for thin marmalade. King George VI, if I may say so without disrespect, like the king in A. A. Milne's famous poem, always did like marmalade at breakfast time. Ever since his young days he had a special liking for a thick Oxford marmalade, and supplies of this were kept at Buckingham Palace and Windsor Castle and taken with us when we moved to any of the other Royal residences. One morning another personal message came to me from the King asking that in future marmalade like that served on the train should be on his breakfast table. Again I made inquiries, and this time solved the problem with ease. The King, so far as I know, never ate his old favorite Oxford marmalade again.

Another of King George VI's particular likes was for a special blend of tea. He drank this with very little milk and just a touch of sugar. At tea the King liked to eat a boiled egg (we had plenty from the Windsor farms) served with a special oriental salt which I have never found outside Buckingham Palace. It was Queen Elizabeth who introduced King George to what became another of his favorite tea dishes, potted shrimps. They were sent direct to the Palace in small aluminium containers from Morecambe Bay in Lancashire, and served on fingers of hot toast. As the third course in the limited austerity lunches and dinners during the war, both the King and Queen used to enjoy small, freshly made cream cheeses which were sent up from time to time from the Royal dairy at Windsor.

There were inquisitive persons who watched everything that went into Buckingham Palace and the other Royal residences in those days of shortage, and I was the innocent and unwitting cause of a rumor that the Royal Family were receiving big extra rations when they were in Scotland.

On our last visit to Balmoral during the war, I arranged as usual for the rationed commodities for the Castle, including those for the Royal Family as well as the Household and staff, to be sent out from the grocer in Aberdeen who had held the Royal Warrant for some years. Because of petrol shortage he could not deliver, as in prewar days, by road, since the Castle is fifty-eight miles from Aberdeen. So after I had telephoned the Royal order and sent the necessary permits with a confirming letter, the goods would be sent by train to Ballater Station, where I would arrange for them to be picked up by one of the Castle shooting brakes. The arrangement worked perfectly all through the war until this very last visit in 1944.

This time the grocer told me when he took my order that he would send everything by rail with the exception of a side of bacon, complete with gammon, and three-quarters of a gross of eggs, for both of which, of course, I had the necessary Ministry of Food permits, as they represented rations for the whole Castle staff. The bacon and eggs, he said, would be sent next day on the Deeside bus. They duly arrived, the bacon done up in sacking, and the eggs in a case labeled for Balmoral Castle. This was enough to set tongues wagging along the whole route from the city to the Castle. So strong was the feeling about this incident that a report appeared in one of the newspapers suggesting that while the war workers had to be content with bread and cheese, there were plenty of eggs and bacon for Royalty. Though there was no basis whatever for the rumors, it was a serious matter, and quickly reached the ears of the King. Later I was questioned closely by the Palace Treasurer about what had happened, and when I made my explanation, a letter was sent, I believe, to the editor of the newspaper setting out the facts.

Queen Elizabeth, the Queen Mother, always took a close interest in the food served at Buckingham Palace and the other residences before, during, and after the war. Like the King, she was—and is—not a big eater, usually taking only two, or at the most, three courses if the menu is a long one. Among her favorite dishes the humble herring, well grilled, takes place beside the more lordly lobster, and she has a liking, too, for oatmeal porridge—a taste deriving, of course, from her Scots blood. She is also fond of fresh fruits, especially strawberries and raspberries, both of which came in plentiful supply to the Royal tables from the fruit gardens at Windsor and Balmoral, the planning and cropping of which she made her personal concern.

Today her daughter, the Queen, follows her mother's example in this, as in so many other ways. She finds time in the midst of her State duties to keep a watchful eye on the produce from Windsor, Sandringham, and Balmoral. Another liking which the Queen shares with her mother is for freshly killed trout, a delicacy frequently served at Balmoral, where the Queen Mother of late years has spent a lot of her time fishing on the banks of the Dee, frequently bringing in her creel two or three silver trout back in triumph to the Castle. These fish are served for dinner that night if she returns in time, but often her keenness as a fisherman outweighs her sense of time, and I have known occasions when she has returned to the Castle from the riverside half an hour or more after the dinner gong has sounded.

I remember once being sent for by Queen Elizabeth, who to my surprise told me that she had heard plaice had been served for the staff lunch.

"They tell me it was excellent," she said. "Where did you get it?"

I told Her Majesty that I had had the fish sent direct from Aberdeen. She asked me to see that when the next consignment came some was served to her—an order which, of course, I was delighted to carry out. But what baffled me was how the Queen had come to know of the menu served to the staff.

Every day the Royal Chef sent up to her—as he does nowadays to the Queen—two or three specimen menus for the Royal table, from which she would choose whichever dishes she preferred for lunch and dinner, marking the chosen items with a penciled tick. But the menu for the staff was a different matter. The items for it were chosen, of course, without consultation with the Queen. Nevertheless, she certainly knew what was going on. I made inquiries and found that the maid to the Queen's lady-in-waiting had so enjoyed her plaice that she went directly after lunch to her mistress to tell her all about it. The lady-in-waiting repeated her maid's remark to the Queen, and the Queen sent for me to hear what it was all about.

Fresh-picked vegetables, especially young broad beans, new peas, and carrots, small lettuce and new potatoes just out of the ground, are favorites with both the Queen Mother and the Queen. Royal gardeners at Windsor have special orders to bring on the spring vegetables early with cloches and frames to supply the Royal table. In the orchards, too, the gardeners tend apple, plum, and pear trees, specially to provide the fruit which is always served after lunch and dinner at Buckingham Palace and at Clarence House. Apricots, nectarines, and peaches are also favorites with Queen Elizabeth. Another of her likings—again shared by her daughter the Queen—is for asparagus. At Sandringham there are a number of very productive beds of this delightful vegetable. It is served at the Royal table either hot with melted butter sauce, or cold with homemade mayonnaise or sauce hollandaise.

Queen Mary, brought up in a more spacious world, had one or two more exotic tastes than her son or daughter-in-law. One of these was for *pâté de foie gras,* the rich paste of goose liver mingled with truffles for which the French town of Strasbourg is renowned. During one of her first visits to Sandringham after her wartime stay at Badminton with the Duke and Duchess of Beaufort, Queen Mary casually remarked to one of her entourage that it seemed a very long time since she had tasted *foie gras.* The King heard of this and he immediately gave orders that a terrine of *pâté* was to be procured and sent to Sandringham.

The order was passed on to me, and I began to search London for the *pâté*, which was in extremely short supply. Eventually I tracked down a supply and asked how much a large terrine would cost. I could have only a small pot containing, perhaps, a quarter of a pound, and this would cost £5. "Much too dear," I said, remembering the economy wave, and sent a message to the King to that effect. Back came an urgent order. I was to get the *pâté* at once and send it immediately to Sandringham. When his mother's wishes were in question, nothing was too difficult or too expensive for King George VI.

King George VI made it a practice throughout his reign not to attend public dinners or lunches in Great Britain unless at Guildhall on some great occasion. When he had attended a civic lunch on his travels up and down the country, he invariably went back to the Royal train to dine, and it is true to say that he did not really enjoy eating out. An exception may be made of the rare cases when he and the Queen went to dine with friends, or the even rarer cases when the King went out alone to attend private informal dinner parties like those of the Garden Society, an association of garden lovers started by his old friend and counselor, Lord Wigram. But during the war, at any rate, hotel food was served at Buckingham Palace at the King's own table.

The explanation of this lies in the food scarcities from which we suffered so badly in those days. Sometimes, despite the supplies of grouse, venison, pheasant, partridge, hare, and other game, the Royal larder would run very low. The King or Queen might ask for a dish which we simply could not produce from the Palace stores. Then I would telephone to my friends in the big hotels and ask them if they had the items we needed. Usually from one or other of them I would find what was wanted, and the dish which the King or Queen had chosen would be served without their being any the wiser as to its origin. More than once when my hotel friends could not help me I turned to a famous public house, the Windsor Castle, near the Palace at Victoria, and several times supplies were sent from this "Castle" to the Royal Palace. I recall a frantic hunt for crabs after the Queen had sent an order to the Chef for dressed crab for lunch at which she and the King were entertaining some foreign guests. Our fish supplier had none. I telephoned half a dozen hotels, and at last persuaded the Dorchester chef to let me have half a dozen of his "on loan." An orderly hurried from the Palace by cycle to collect the fish just in time.

I have often been asked why it was that King George VI did not follow his father's example and declare the Royal residences teetotal for the duration of the war. It was certainly not because of any great fondness by the King and Queen for alcoholic drink. King George VI drank very sparingly indeed, usually only a small whisky before dinner and another with his meal, with perhaps a third as a final nightcap. The main reason was that the King thought that the depressing effect of being deprived of a little stimulant in the shape of whisky, wine, or beer would outweigh the possible advantages of depriving his staff of alcohol altogether, as he knew in advance from his Ministers that many things would be in short supply, and that in any case there would not be enough whisky to encourage or allow overindulgence.

When the King and Queen traveled, as they so often did during the war, on the Royal train, known then for security reasons as "The Grove Special," the food was supplied by the railway companies. But there were certain extras which the King liked which could be supplied only from Buckingham Palace, and it was my job to arrange that these foodstuffs were always put on the Royal train in advance. Small, round cream cheeses sent up every day from the Royal dairy at Windsor formed one important item on this list. Another was half a pound of butter made into pats, and a dozen fresh eggs, also from the same dairy. One other important item was a small tin containing the Earl Grey tea which the King invariably drank. Another item which we were never called upon to supply to King George VI, but which had been a regular feature in the days of King George V, was plovers' eggs. When George V was on the throne plovers' eggs were sent up every day in the season to the Royal table. King George V enjoyed eating them very much indeed, but King George VI did not.

When King George VI and Queen Elizabeth went to Windsor Castle to take up their residence there for the first time, there was much speculation about what would happen to the two Princesses, whether they would be "parked out" at Royal Lodge, or whether they would be included in the Royal house party. We were not left long in doubt. The Queen, we found, never liked to be separated from her children longer than was absolutely necessary. So the Princesses came to Windsor Castle for the Ascot visit too, though naturally they did not go anywhere near the racecourse. They took up their quarters in the nursery suite in the Victoria Tower with their Nannie, the late Mrs. Knight, two nursemaids, and a young footman, to attend to their wants.

They led a very regular life, keeping strictly to the timetable laid down for them by the Queen. Breakfast for five— the two Princesses, Mrs. Knight, and the two nursemaids— was served at 8 A.M. They got up quarter past seven, dressed, washed, and were ready for breakfast before eight, having already said their morning prayers. Luncheon for five was sent up exactly at 1 P.M. This was a light meal with those plainly cooked dishes which the Queen thought best for her children. Both were good eaters and there were never complaints of "leftovers" from the Royal nursery lunch table. At four-thirty tea was sent up with bread and butter, jam, plain biscuits, and usually some cake. In the evening there were two meals. The Princesses had a light snack with a sweet at seven o'clock, then their Nannie and the two nursemaids would be served with a normal evening meal about an hour and a half later, when the children had been put to bed.

I remember the first birthday that Princess Elizabeth spent at Windsor Castle in April, 1937. The King's Pastry Cook, delighted at the chance to display his skill, baked a special fruit cake, finished off with a chocolate covering decorated with white icing sugar and the simple wording "Happy Birthday" with the date April 21, 1937, beneath. This cake, mounted on the usual circular three-ply board covered with silver paper, was taken up to the nursery for Royal tea on the Princess's birthday. The King and Queen joined their daughters for their birthday tea and the cake was pronounced a great success. For the three following days the cake was sent up at teatime! A large iced presentation cake was always delivered to Windsor Castle by a well-known firm of biscuit manufacturers for the Princess's birthday. This would arrive in a large van, accompanied by two of the firm's directors and the chef who had made the cake, with one or two of his assistants, so that unloading the Princess's presentation birthday cake from the van was quite a ceremony. Usually the cake was made in three tiers, and these would be carried into the Royal kitchens one at a time. The chef and his assistants would closely inspect each of the tiers, and if any of the intricate sugar work had been broken in transit they would bring out their piping bags and repair the damage before the cake was taken along the corridors to the lift which would convey it up to the Nursery Floor. It was always set up on a

sideboard in the Nursery Sitting Room where the two Princesses could admire it during the day.

I have known our own Pastry Chef to come into the stores
and stand lost in admiration at the work in the presentation
cake. Sometimes he would look very downcast and disappointed, comparing the beautiful intricate work on the presentation cake with his own plainer efforts. "The Princess
won't want my little cake when she sees that," he would say,
almost in tears. But every year it was the homemade cake
which the Princess ate first.

She and her sister always ate some of the presentation cake,
but most of this was cut into large wedges for the local hospitals, the Officers' Mess of the Guards Barracks at Windsor,
and the remainder would be cut into small portions to be
issued to each member of the Castle staff.

One of the great sources of food supplies for Buckingham
Palace is the Royal gardens and farms at Windsor, Balmoral,
and Sandringham. Strangely enough, though it has seven
acres of grounds around it, Buckingham Palace has no kitchen
garden of its own, and all the vegetables and fruit from the
Royal gardens come to the Palace from Windsor. They are delivered each morning in a dark-blue-painted motorcar with
the Royal Crown and the words "Royal Gardens—Windsor"
on the sides.

Whether food comes from the Royal garden at Windsor or
from Covent Garden or from the fruiterer's shop at Victoria
Station, run by an Australian friend of mine who is himself
the possessor of a Royal Warrant, every item, whether it is
a humble cabbage, a lettuce, a pound of fresh strawberries, or
a bunch of new asparagus, is carefully checked and entered
into the books.

The weight, price, and size of all items are also entered into
these books. Bookkeeping is nowadays a major occupation at

Buckingham Palace, for, as I mentioned earlier, the Palace is now run on strict business lines.

When King George V was on the throne, in my early days at the Palace, the place was run as a gentleman's household, without too nice regard to economy or finance.

In those more spacious and freer days there was a greater liberality everywhere. Food and drink were plentiful and no one seemed to mind much exactly how much they cost. Today all that has been changed. It is, indeed, twenty years or more since the luxury days of free spending began to disappear from the Palace life. Now every item is entered, checked, and costed, and the accounts are made up to pennies. Indeed, the cost-of-living figures for the food supplied to members of the Royal Household, to officials and servants, are worked out to such a degree of accuracy that they are calculated to two decimals of a penny per head.

This system of accounting involved me in one of my most important—and interesting—jobs, which was nothing less than working out to fractions of a penny just how much the King and Queen were spending on their food day by day, budgeting for them not to exceed their daily "allowance," and generally trying to make the Palace "pay," just as though we were in fact running the big hotel to which I so often compared the place.

This is how the system worked. Each week we had a thorough stocktaking of all food, perishables, and stores in the larders and cold room as a basis for a weekly and monthly food costing which I worked out, one for the officials and staff, the other for the Royal Family and Household. These were arrived at by bringing the value of the foodstuffs in the Royal kitchen and stores forward and adding to that total the amount of receipts (from the Chef) given in during the week, less the stock on hand at the weekend, thus giving the total amount of food consumed during the seven days. After that it was a matter of simple division to find the cost per person per meal. This multiplied by four (breakfast, lunch, tea, and dinner) gave the cost per person per day—and the figures had to be calculated to two decimal points of a penny, as I have said. The King was so keen on this procedure that after a trial period at Buckingham Palace it was adopted at Windsor Castle and the other Royal residences.

It was a great change indeed from the carefree spending of my early days at the Palace, and indicates more than anything else the conversion of the Sovereign's residence from a private gentleman's home to another department of State or the Civil Service.

Up to 1953, the cost for the Royal Family and Household was 25s. to 30s. a day per person, the figure for officials and staff 5s. 6d. to 6s. So, you see, the King's house was, and the Queen's house is, run on business lines, with every penny of outgoings accounted for, as in any well-run hotel. In hotels the income from receipts for meals is balanced against the cost of producing the meals to arrive at the profit or loss and what is known as the "kitchen percentage." At the Palace, of course, we had no actual cash receipts to use as a balance. Instead, we used an assessed figure for the Royal meals, agreed in advance by the Privy Purse authorities, and set the actual cost of the meals against this figure, giving us a percentage above or below, indicating a "loss" or a "profit."

In 1952 and at the start of 1953 the Royal costs were outrunning the assessed figure week after week, and there was more than a little concern at the resulting expenditure curve. I had to have several talks with the Chef to see if he could put forward any ideas for saving costs. But he said flatly that he saw no way of bringing down costs when all prices were rising, unless we wanted to lower the standard of food served, which I knew the Queen would not tolerate for a moment. The basis of the Chef's argument, and I must say I entirely agreed with him, was the low estimate of the figure laid down by the Deputy-Treasurer to the Queen, a former naval officer, for the Royal table. His figures totaled 15s. a day, made up as follows: Royal calling tray, 6d.; Royal breakfast, 2s. 6d.; Royal lunch, 5s. 6d.; Royal tea, 1s.; and Royal dinner, 5s. 6d. We both, with much practical experience of buying food, thought these figures inadequate, as indeed they proved in practice to be. All this was not due to any meanness on the part of King George VI, or today, of Queen Elizabeth II. It is merely part of the new pattern of Royal living, in which every effort is made to keep the Palace on a firm and proper business basis so that the Sovereign does not have to dip constantly into reserves of money, as King George V had to do time and time again, to balance the accounts.

In those days many members of the Royal Household were gentlemen who had little, if any, business training. They regarded (and the King quite approved of their attitude) their jobs as positions of honor in which they had nothing to do except see that things were kept running smoothly. Such sordid considerations as pennies or shillings did not enter their minds. Today every official of the Royal Household, however high his or her birth, is an expert in his or her own particular field. I suppose the general manager of Buckingham Palace Limited, if you could call it a "firm," as we in the Royal service often referred to it, is the Master of the Household. This post—the most responsible position in many ways on the domestic side of the Palace—is now held by Major Millbank. For many years the late Sir Piers Legh was Master. A Guards Colonel of medium height, who had been in the service of the Duke of Windsor when he was Prince of Wales, Sir Piers was a man of some shortness of temper. He was not the most popular of figures among the servants, to whom, as to members of the Royal Household and to the Royal Family themselves, he was invariably known, for some entirely obscure reason, as "Joey." But short-tempered or not, "Joey" was a first-class administrator, and nothing ever went really wrong at Buckingham Palace in his day. He could tick off an erring servant with all the vigor of a Guards officer, and a few minutes later be as sympathetic and kindly as a man could be to any member of the staff who was in trouble or distress.

The Master of the Household is responsible directly to the Sovereign for all the domestic servants in the Palace. It is also his responsibility to see that everything needed for the proper maintenance and running of the Palace is there—food, household linen, furniture, etc. To help him, the Master has a staff of perhaps one hundred and twenty, including minor officials, clerks, secretaries, and menservants, with about another eighty or a hundred women servants, including kitchen cleaners and so on.

Equally, if not more, important to the Palace hierarchy is the Keeper of the Privy Purse, at present Lord Tryon. For many years Sir Ulick Alexander—like Lord Tryon and Sir Piers, a Guards officer—held this onerous post, whose duties include keeping a watchful eye on the whole of the Royal finances, the Sovereign's personal expenditure, as well as all the salaries of the Household, and all the costs of running the Palace. The Keeper is a sort of private Chancelor of the Exchequer to the Sovereign, or, to continue the business allegory, he is the secretary and treasurer of the company.

One feature of Buckingham Palace little suspected by those who stand peering in through the railings at the Guardchanging, or who watch the Queen drive out on some visit, is that the four sides of the Palace buildings have a replica underground. Here, perhaps twenty feet below surface, there is a self-contained village which supplies all the Royal needs that can be met from within. As you go along the corridors you pass painters' shops, wine cellars, food stores, a plumber's shop, cabinetmakers, carpentry shops, and many other tradesmen, all playing their part in the maintenance of the Palace. Many of the men who work in these places are not members of the Royal staff, but are on the payroll of the Ministry of Works specially attached to Buckingham Palace. Supervising a great number of these is the Superintendent of the Palace, a position which does not rank in the Royal Household itself, but which carries with it the responsibility for maintenance and upkeep of all the furniture and valuable period pieces, the china, the paintings, and other "museum" features of the Palace. Mr. Stanley Williams, who at present holds this post, is the son of a man who held it for some forty years. He is not only a personal friend of members of the Royal Family, but himself ranks as an expert on the Royal collection. There is also a senior official of the Ministry of Works permanently in residence at Buckingham Palace, as well as an engineer with a complete staff under him responsible for keeping the boilers and furnaces of the Palace working. In recent years, during the latter part of the reign of King George VI, the whole of the Palace central-heating system was renewed. Oil-burning furnaces were installed in place of the old costly and rather inefficient solid-fuel-burning types, and the Palace today is a warmer, cosier, and more comfortable place altogether than it was when I first went into it as a boy, some twenty-odd years ago.

I have said that there is a village under the Palace. Like most villages it has its village "pub." This, at Buckingham Palace, is on two floors. The "public bar" is in the Servants' Hall on the ground floor, the "saloon bar" is in the Steward's Room, one floor higher up. At either of these places beer, spirits, sherry, and wine can be obtained by members of the staff, and there they may buy drinks for their friends, provided they have had the requisite permission for bringing them in. In the war days the bar of the Steward's Room was a wonderful spot at which to meet heroes. After the Investitures which King George VI held in the Grand Hall on the ground floor, officials would sometimes bring winners of the Victoria Cross or the George Cross, and other distinguished men from the Services, round to the Steward's Room to "have a quick one." I have heard several V.C.'s confess that while they did not remember being frightened when they were winning their decorations, they really "had the wind up" just before they went to bow to their King, and a large whisky afterward was exactly what they needed.

In a section apart are the Buckingham Palace Police. They are all members of the Metropolitan Police Force, and belong to the crack "A" Division with its headquarters in Cannon Row, adjoining Scotland Yard. But the Palace has its own Inspector and also its own Superintendent, who is the Sovereign's personal bodyguard. This police officer is not only in constant attendance on the Sovereign wherever he or she may go, but is also responsible for the administration of all the police at Buckingham Palace and wherever else the Royal Family may be in residence. Some of the Palace Police, known as the "traveling staff," go with the Queen to Balmoral, Sandringham, Windsor, or anywhere else. There are special guards at night, and special secret precautions are taken to ensure that no intruder, even if he or she succeeded in getting into Buckingham Palace itself, could possibly penetrate to the Royal apartments. In recent years police dogs have been introduced into the grounds of the Palace, and the number of times when intruders have got over the walls has fallen to a very small figure.

Whenever anyone does succeed in getting into the Palace grounds there is a full-scale inquiry by a board set up at Scotland Yard, and woe betide the unfortunate holder of the responsible position of Police Officer to the Sovereign if any intruder is shown to have got in through lack of police surveillance. One of the most difficult periods for the police in this respect is when there are garden parties or other functions which bring in outside workmen to erect marquees and so on in the Palace gardens. Normally all the Palace staff, servants, and others who come in through the Trade Gate or the Electricians' Gate are well known by sight to the police. They all carry passes, but are very rarely, if ever, required to show them. When, however, a number of new people, casual laborers, come into the Palace, even though they have all been carefully "vetted" beforehand and issued with passes, it is impossible for the police to recognize them by their faces. They are stopped and asked for their passes, of course, but occasionally a stranger may slip in. After one or two incidents of this kind in recent years, extra precautions were evolved and are now always taken on these occasions to make completely sure that no one, with good intentions or bad, can get into Buckingham Palace without authorization.

Familiarity, even with a palace, breeds, if not contempt, a certain difference of attitude. The men and women whose place of work is Buckingham Palace look on the King's residence in much the same way as you probably look on your office—as the place where there is a job to be done without worrying too much about the surroundings in which you have to do it. Actually there is at Buckingham Palace a very good spirit among all the different sections of the big community who live there to work for their Sovereign. Things do not always run smoothly in such a big organization, however, and there are bound to be occasional clashes of temperament between members of the staff, though any "prima donna" behavior by foreign chefs, or anyone else, was strongly frowned upon. I remember very vividly my own first serious clash with a member of the Household, and I still feel, after all these years, that I was in the right.

It was at Balmoral, during one of the wartime visits, that the Queen gave me orders to arrange for a dance in a couple of days' time, and told me she would send the invitation list down to me later that day. I had a busy time arranging refreshments, ordering the band, writing and sending out the invitations, and it was midnight before I had finished. I thought this was a long enough day, and went up to my room certain that no one would disturb me that night. How wrong I was! I had been in bed some twenty minutes when there was a knock on the door and a footman called out to me that the Equerry on duty wanted to see me in the billiard room. I answered that he could tell the Equerry that I was in bed. Next morning the Equerry sent for me and gave me a thorough telling-off for not coming at his call. I answered back, standing up for myself, and told him I thought from eight in the morning to midnight in the office was a fair day's work. We parted on bad terms, but I thought that on reflection he would see my point and no more would be heard of the matter. Not a bit of it. He telephoned a complaint to Windsor Castle about my conduct. I still took no notice, until I received a letter from my chief (and friend), James Kennedy, asking me not to throw away the years of good work I had put in, but to go and apologize. This I had no inclination to do, but J. K. told me there was so strong a feeling in the Household, that I would have no chance in a showdown. Whether this was so or not I never found out, for I reluctantly took his advice. But I had not the same respect for that particular Equerry afterward.

The Palace community is split into rigorously defined sections. Next to the Sovereign and the Royal Family come the Royal Household, with their own dining room—which is now used on occasions as the private cinema for the Queen and her family—and their own rest rooms. Next in rank are the officials, who include people who hold various posts such as accountants, clerks, and secretaries. They eat in a room of their own and have their own recreation rooms.

Next to them are the upper-servants who eat in the Steward's Room with the more junior servants—though not necessarily in terms of age—below them eating in the Servants' Hall.

It is a complete social pyramid in itself at Buckingham Palace and here, if nowhere else in the world today, the lines are rigidly drawn. It is absolutely forbidden for a servant, for instance, from the Steward's Room to go into the Officials' Mess except on some very special occasion, and no official would dream of intruding into the Household Dining Room any more than members of the Royal Household would dream of barging into the Sovereign's dining room.

At Sandringham, Windsor, and Balmoral things are different in one particular. At these places the Sovereign always dines and lunches with members of his or her Household. But at Buckingham Palace the Royal Family keep strictly to themselves.

I have said the Palace is like a hotel. It is a hotel with a very small, select, but permanent clientele. Only at times like the Coronation, or on State visits of foreign Royalty, does the hotel really fill up. All along the front of Buckingham Palace on the second and third floors are guest rooms for foreign visitors and their staffs and suites. When these are filled, then indeed the hotel is busy, and everyone at the Palace works almost the whole day.

When King George VI wanted to find out what economies

he could make in the running of the Palace in 1948, it was for a hotel chief that he sent to give him advice. Mr. Hugh Wontner, of the Savoy Hotel, came to Buckingham Palace and for six weeks lived with us and studied our methods and our ways. At the end he reported to the King, "There is nothing very much I can do." We all thought that that was a great tribute to the way we had been working.

As in any other hotel, one of the most important people in the Palace retinue is a little-heard-of and very rarely seen person, the housekeeper. For many years this post was held by my old friend Mrs. Ferguson, now retired.

Mrs. Ferguson, a good Scot, like so many of the men and women employed at Buckingham Palace, is a woman who was never perturbed by any circumstances that might arise. I have seen her, calm and unflurried, in the midst of the bustle and preparation for a State visit at Buckingham Palace, when even the King and Queen have been a little concerned as to whether things were going to come out right. But "Fergie" was always calm. Harassed housemaids would rush up to her with stories that there was no linen for so-and-so's bedroom, that the towel supplies had run out, or with some similar minor household crisis. Fergie was always equal to the occasion. This quality of calmness was one which appealed particularly to the Queen. They were great friends, and many is the time I have heard from Fergie's own lips in her room on the ground floor of the Palace, at the end of a tiring day, of what she and the Queen had been talking about, and how the Queen had asked her advice, particularly in the beginning of the reign of George VI, about various domestic matters. Queen Elizabeth, the Queen Mother, and her daughter, the present Queen, both have a great affection for Scots. Fergie has now been succeeded by Mrs. Findlater. Like Fergie, Mrs. Findlater is a maiden lady. It is in accordance with an old-fashioned custom of "below stairs" that the housekeeper at any big house, whether she be married or not, is always referred to as "Mrs."

At the head of the men's household, indeed heading all the servants at Buckingham Palace, is the Palace Steward. For the whole of the reign of King George VI this post was filled by Mr. Ainslie, who had been the King's butler when, as Duke of York, the King was living at 145 Piccadilly. Like Mrs. Ferguson, Ainslie was imperturbable—at least on the surface. But unlike her he sometimes showed his emotions in private. Tall, suave, always immaculately dressed, the acme of self-contained efficiency, Ainslie has always seemed to me to be the ideal of an English butler. In Buckingham Palace the Royal machine must always work with the absolute quintessence of smoothness. It is a Palace rule—as I was told, I think, on my first day there—that "nothing must go wrong here. Mistakes are never made." One of the most important parts of Ainslie's job was to see that mistakes were never made. Yet occasionally things did go wrong.

King George VI was not a man of the most even temper, especially in his younger days, and I have known occasions when some hitch has occurred, perhaps in the service of a meal, and the King's annoyance would be aroused. Inevitably he would direct it against Ainslie, though he was not personally at fault. It was some under-servant who had erred. Ainslie never complained. He took his Royal master's wrath as it came; then, in private later, told off the erring servant. But I have seen him shaken and moved, because he had a great affection for the King, as well as an enormous respect for the Royal Household and pride in the job that he was performing. For things to go wrong worried him almost as much as it worried his Royal master.

On occasions like these, though they were happily few and

far between, it was the Queen—Queen Elizabeth, the Queen Mother—who smoothed things over. Her effect on King George VI was almost magical. I have seen the late King in angry mood over something, his eyes gleaming. Then the Queen has uttered one or two words to him and suddenly his anger has dissolved and turned to laughter. There was no one else in the Royal circle who could produce this effect on the King until the last few years of his life, when Princess Elizabeth, now our Queen, and Princess Margaret, both seemed to have inherited something of their mother's ability to soothe the ruffled feelings of their father.

Smoothly though the Royal machine may work, there are problems at Buckingham Palace beneath the surface. Today, particularly, there are labor problems. In the old days, when I first went to the Palace, there was a special field of recruitment for menservants for the Royal service. They came from the big houses inhabited by the great noblemen who maintained large staffs. Some of these, like the late Earl of Granard, Master of the Horse, had as part of the duties deriving from their Court appointments the task of training servants for the Palace. Young country lads would go to the great houses and there enter into service as junior footmen. When they had been sufficiently trained, if they were good enough, their names would be forwarded by their nobleman-employer to the Master of the King's Household, who would take them on for a trial period.

Nearly all the servants who were at the Palace throughout the reign of George VI started in this way. This training produced a very loyal, discreet, and lovable type of servant, whose interests were closely identified with those of his Royal master, and who had almost as much respect for the institution of the Monarchy as the King himself. Today, with very few large country estates left, and fewer still with any big staffs maintained on them, this source of supply has almost entirely disappeared. Now Buckingham Palace has to rely for its labor supply, as other firms and businesses do, on recruitment from youths often almost straight from school. It takes years for them to be thoroughly trained as Royal servants and their inexperience throws a strain on the older men, which some of them are inclined to resent. Nor do these younger men have the same traditions of loyalty and discretion as the older servants. Many of them come to Buckingham Palace for perhaps six months or a year, then leave and trade on their reputation as having been "in the service of the Queen." Neither is it only among the servants that there is a certain amount of labor trouble. When I first went to the Palace the women confidential clerks who act as secretaries to the Queen's Secretary and the other high officials of the Household were nearly all recruited from the upper-middle classes. Many of them were girls with small private incomes of their own with which to supplement the somewhat meager payment from the Palace. They could have earned much more elsewhere, but preferred to work at the Palace because of the social prestige it brought, and also because of certain particular prerogatives reserved for members of the Royal Household staff.

Many of these prerogatives remain today. For instance, everyone at Buckinham Palace is allowed to go to the Royal Race Meeting at Ascot in June. Servants have passes which take them and their friends to the roof of the Royal stand, where one of the most wonderful views of racing in this country can be obtained. Members of the Household staff, the lady clerks and others, have passes for the grandstand and paddock, though not, of course, to the Royal Enclosure. In prewar days these social amenities were an added attraction to persuade people to come to the Royal service. There was also the prospect of a good pension. In those days there were few jobs with pensions, whereas today, with pensions for practically all jobs, and at higher rates than the Palace pays, the attraction of working for the Royal Family is nothing like so great. To prove this point I may say that in the first fifteen years of my service at Buckingham Palace I can recall no woman clerk leaving, except in one or two instances where they went to get married. In the last five or six years I was at the Palace there was almost a constant procession of women who came and worked for a short period and then left.

The alteration in the methods of recruitment of men and women for the Royal service creates other problems, particularly in the field of security. Just after the war, when the Palace staff was being built up again to its former proportions, and many newcomers were taken on, in some cases the references were not fully gone into and checked. I recall, for example, the case of a young woman who was taken on and went into Clarence House to become a clerk in the household of the newly married Princess Elizabeth. Her references were of the highest. She claimed to come from county society. All seemed well, and she was certainly an efficient worker. Then one day she did not turn up for duty. Nor did she arrive the next day or the day after. She had just walked out, leaving behind her a trail of debts to her fellow-clerks, to some of the servants, and to some members of the Princess's household, totaling £200 or £300. The police were discreetly called in and told to make inquiries. It was found that her references were entirely false, that she did not come from a county family, but was, in fact, the daughter of a small shopkeeper in South London who was in ignorance of his daughter's pretensions or of the fact that she had worked at Clarence House.

One of the most noticeable changes at Buckingham Palace today compared with the days when I first went there is in the liveries worn by the Royal servants. In my early days each servant wore every day a stiff white shirt like an evening shirt, with an upright collar and a white evening tie. The upper-servants wore dark-blue tailcoats lined with silk, with gilt buttons bearing the Royal cipher. The under-servants wore similar coats in scarlet cloth, heavily embroidered with gold wire, with black waistcoats also embroidered in gold. The cost of laundering the servants' white shirts, collars, and ties was a heavy item in the Privy Purse accounts, and both King George V in the latter years of his reign, and after him King George VI, wondered how they could cut out this recurrent expenditure. Nothing, apparently, could be done, but during the war there was the necessity for cutting down laundry, and King George VI applied his mind to the problem and solved it. He himself designed a new form of Royal livery, on battle-dress lines, based largely on the uniforms he had seen worn by the Westminster Civil Defense men. One of these uniforms was sent to Balmoral Castle, and I had it taken to the King for his inspection.

King George VI was very interested in the details of all uniforms and equipment, and spent a long time drawing designs to adapt the Civil Defense coat to the purposes of a Royal livery. The eventual design consisted of a battledress blouse on military lines, secured at the waist by the usual strap and buckle, with a large GR VI cipher on the left-hand pocket of the blouse, epaulet cords fixed over both shoulders, and large gilt buttons, also bearing the cipher, down the center of the tunic. The King also went into details of the cut of the trousers, which were specially designed so as to make a neat seat. Several trial-and-error suits were made before the King was satisfied, and the order went to a London firm of tailors to fit all the Pages and footmen with the new livery. The Pages and other senior servants had their ciphers and shoulder straps in gilt wire, whereas the lower servants had red ciphers with red shoulder cords. So successful was the King's design that this livery is the everyday wear at the Palace today.

Full State livery is still worn very occasionally at Buckingham Palace by the Queen's menservants—on such occasions as the Coronation, or the State visit of any foreign Royalty. One of the Royal servants in his State dress is indeed a magnificent sight. The livery coat, blue again for the senior servants, red for the others, is a very heavy affair, profusely embroidered in real gold wire worked into designs and bearing the Royal cipher. The tunic weighs some twenty-five pounds and is worth at least £40. With these tunics, knee breeches and white silk stockings with buckled shoes are worn, and every man in State livery must have his hair powdered in the old-fashioned style. Buckingham Palace is probably the only place in Great Britain where you may still, on occasion, see menservants with properly powdered hair. Each male newcomer to the Palace service is taught this difficult art. The hair is powdered with ordinary flour, and a practiced hand can do his hair in twenty minutes, whereas a beginner will take perhaps three-quarters of an hour.

All the servants at Buckingham Palace are the proud possessors of many medals; nearly all of them now have the medals of the last war or of the First World War, and in addition to these are many other decorations given to them either by the British Sovereign or by foreign Royalties who have visited the Palace and on whom they have been in waiting. In full State livery the large-size medals are worn, adding glowing color to the whole.

There were no eight-hour days for Royal servants at Buckingham Palace—they must be on duty all day. But to make up for this there is a system of days off, so that one servant may work the whole day, sleep at the Palace that night, work the next day, and then be off for a couple of days while his colleague who has had two days off takes his place. The system works very well, and there is little real discontent among the men and women employed at the Palace, though today they are nearly all members of a trade union, the Civil Service Union—something which King George V would never have tolerated, for though he was a keen supporter of the rights of labor, he believed that his servants were personal employees of his own, with whom he always maintained a friendly though distant relationship. He paid them and looked after their well-being. Although in those days there were many men and women in the Royal service who never saw the King or Queen from one year's end to another, King George V and Queen Mary knew all their servants by name, and Queen Mary, particularly, would always inquire after the health of any one of them who was missing from his or her post for a day or two. She would arrange for flowers or gifts of food and delicacies to be dispatched with a message of cheer from her—a Royal touch which delighted the invalids. Today everything is done on rather more official lines.

One of the most important servants at the Palace is the valet to the King, or the maid to the Queen. When I first came to Buckingham Palace, and all through the rest of the reign of King George V, one of the most influential men "below stairs" was Richard Howlett, the King's valet. In appearance like an ambassador, with a courtly manner and a gentle voice, Howlett was indeed a power in the land, if not behind the throne. King George V placed great reliance on the wisdom and judgment of this man, who had been his personal servant over a period of many years. He gave him a very lovely apartment at St. James's Palace for his home and treated him as a confidant, almost as a friend. There were people who suggested that Howlett had more influence over the King on certain matters than he really should have had.

King George VI, when he came to the throne, was very conscious of this. He determined that nothing of the kind should be said about him and his valet, Tom Jerram. So though Tom, who has been a close friend of mine for many years, was on terms of considerable intimacy with his Royal master, there was never any suggestion of influence. Tom, of course, shared many of the King's secrets, but he was never known to reveal any of them. Talkative and friendly on such matters as racing and sport, he would close up like an oyster if anyone started to ask him anything about the King.

King George VI, always immaculately turned out and taking great pride in his personal appearance, owed a good deal to the ministrations of Tom Jerram, who would work far into the night in order to produce his Royal master's clothes, particularly the uniforms of the three Services, which were the King's constant wear during the war, in perfect condition. One of his especial prides was the polishing of the King's shoes and Sam Browne belt. The King used to say, laughingly, that he had the finest polish on his shoes of any officer in the three Services.

Today Miss Margaret MacDonald—known affectionately by the Queen, and by everyone else at Buckingham Palace, as "Bo-bo," from the Queen's childish efforts to pronounce her name when she was nursery maid at 145 Piccadilly—enjoys the position of being the Queen's closest confidante as well as her personal maid. It is Bo-bo who calls the Queen every morning at 8:15 with her morning cup of tea. It is Bo-bo who tends to the vast details of her Royal mistress's dresses. It is Bo-bo who hears the Queen's comments on many people and many things. But, like Tom, Bo-bo is never to be drawn into conversation about the Queen.

What happens to Royal servants when they leave the Palace? In the old days they would stay in the service until the age for retirement came, and you may still see at Windsor, Sandringham, and elsewhere elderly men and women who live in "grace-and-favor" cottages and flats, rent free, as part of their pensions, and who could, if they would, tell you fascinating stories of bygone days in the Royal house. Today many of the young servants who have been at the Palace for only a short time leave to seek other employment. One who had been in the Royal service for about ten years went out to New Zealand, where he is now a successful dairy farmer. Many others, having left the Royal service, take up posts in the West End catering firms, which specialize in catering for outside parties.

One of the most important, indeed the only direct, means of communication, apart from broadcasting, between the King or Queen and his or her subjects is the Court Circular— that official announcement of Royal activities which is issued not every day but most days from Buckingham Palace. It is because this is the only direct way the Sovereign can communicate with people that the Court Circular is always made the medium for announcing Royal engagements. It is prepared at Buckingham Palace by the clerk to the Master of the Household, a retired Paymaster Lieutenant Commander of the Royal Navy. Each evening the draft of the Court Circular is sent up for the Queen's personal approval. If she wishes to alter any word of it she will do so in blue pencil and then send it back to the clerk who transmits it to the news agencies for sending to the newspapers. Up at Balmoral and at Sandringham the duty of writing out the Court Circular used to form part of my duties, and many a worrying evening I have had making sure that I had spelled each name correctly and got the correct order of precedence. Otherwise King George VI would be angry with me, and to have the King angry with you was no pleasant experience.

It was in the Court Circular routine that King George VI made one of the few alterations in the Balmoral regime from his father's time. Under King George V the name of every guest at Balmoral, whatever his or her position might be, had to be included in the Court Circular. It was when King Edward VIII put the name of Mrs. Simpson in his Court Circular that the troubles which led to the abdication really came to a head. Perhaps because of this, King George VI decided that the names of his guests should not appear in the Court Circular, and this practice has been followed by Queen Elizabeth II.

As an example of the attention to detail which has to be given to the arrangement of every Royal function, here is what happens before a dinner party at Buckingham Palace, or every night at Balmoral or Sandringham when the Queen is entertaining guests. The name of each person is typewritten on two small cards. These cards are then sorted into two batches, ladies and gentlemen, and together sent up to the Queen with what is called the dinner board. The Queen places the cards in slots on the board, representing the position at the table where she wants her guests to be seated. At about eight o'clock—half an hour before dinner is served—the board is brought back to one of the officials, who takes it up and places it in the drawing room, so that the guests when they come in may see where they are to sit. The other cards are placed round the table itself, in each case just above the sweet spoon and fork where the guest will be sitting. Everything, down to the last detail, has to be thought out in advance and all possibilities taken into account.

The men and women who work for the Queen are ordinary folk just like you and me. Once the Royal servants have taken off their livery and come out of the Trade Gate into busy, bustling Buckingham Palace Road, they are lost in the crowd with nothing to pick them out from the other men and women who work for different masters. The Royal servants do their bit of gardening, enjoy their game of cricket or football, visit the local pub, or go to the pictures just as we do. There is one difference. Their employer is their Queen, and even in these days when, as I have said, the old traditions are not quite the same, every one of the people who work at Buckingham Palace is proud to be able to say, "I work for my Queen." That is about all they will say, or indeed are allowed to say, about their work. One thing that annoys the Queen more than anything else is to find in the newspapers reports about what she considers to be her private life. If these reports are inaccurate it annoys her but if they are accurate it annoys her even more, for it means that there is a "leak."

Experts on the Constitution have written learned treatises to prove that one of the reasons why we still have a Monarchy in Great Britain today, when so many other countries have lost theirs, is that the British Monarchy has always known how to adapt itself to changing conditions. What truth there may be in this I do not claim to know, but I do know that I have seen many changes at Buckingham Palace in my own time from the days of George V to the early days of Queen Elizabeth II. Nearly all these changes have tended to a more democratic approach by the Palace and to closer, more personal relationships between the Sovereign and the people. This contact really starts between the Sovereign and the men and women who serve him or her. I think that one of the most obvious examples of King George's democratization of Buckingham Palace lies in the annual staff dances that are now a regular feature of the Royal Christmas festivities. These dances, one of which takes place at Windsor Castle and the others at Buckingham Palace, are occasions when the men and women who serve the Sovereign can dance with the Queen and members of her family as their partners. This is something that King George V and Queen Mary would never have dreamed of doing.

The first of the staff dances was held at the wish of King George VI in the last year of the war, at Windsor Castle. These dances are organized by the Royal Household Staff Canteen Fund. They are run entirely by the Royal servants, without any interference or direction from the members of the Royal Family or the Household officials. At Windsor the Queen, following her father's tradition, allows her servants to have the use of the famous Waterloo Chamber for their dance. At Buckingham Palace they use the Ball Supper Room, with its wonderful array of five rose crystal chandeliers, and its beautifully inlaid polished floor on which debutantes walk to make their curtsies to the Queen. The Waterloo Chamber at Windsor, incidentally, is so called because on its walls hang pictures of the Duke of Wellington and the other leaders who helped Britain and her allies to conquer and overthrow Napoleon. It was in this room that the present Queen, as Princess Elizabeth, appeared with her sister, Princess Margaret, in the pantomimes which they wrote during the wartime Christmases.

Each of the Royal servants is allowed to bring one guest to the staff dance. For this occasion they put off their livery and don lounge suits or afternoon dresses. The servants and their friends gather in the Waterloo Chamber or the State Ballroom at about half-past eight, and dance to music from one of the well-known West End bands. About an hour later there is an interval, and the Queen, with the Duke of Edinburgh, and perhaps Princess Margaret and the Queen Mother, walk in in full evening dress. The Queen and members of her family take the floor, each partnered by one of the servants or the staff. These partners are selected beforehand by a committee of the staff social club and their names submitted to the Queen for her approval. But even so, the Queen, or one member of the Royal Family, will go up to one of the servants and ask him or her for a dance—a Royal gesture of recognition that really delights the man or woman to whom it is made.

I well remember the first of these affairs at Windsor. I was there with my wife, and eager to see how things would go. This time the band was from the local detachment of the Royal Air Force, and a very good band it was. Next to the Waterloo Chamber is a room known as the Garter Chamber, because here the Garter Knights assemble when there is a Chapter of that Most Noble Order (Chapter means a ceremonial meeting at which the Sovereign of the Order will install new Knights).

These dances, and many other amenities the Royal servants enjoy, are paid for out of the profits of the Staff Canteen, an institution started in the days of George V, but which owes its continued existence to the interest and help of George VI. When he came to the Palace in 1937, the Canteen, where members of the staff, from officers of the Household to kitchen porters and scullery maids, could buy port, sherry, whisky, beer, cigarettes, and other items at less than outside retail prices, was in a bad state financially. Though it was open every day and doing brisk business, the losses steadily grew larger, owing to the low prices charged. Whisky was 10s. 6d. a bottle; gin, 10s.; fine port and sherry, 3s. 9d.—absurdly cheap even for those days. But King George V did not see why anything connected with the Palace should be run for profit, and so things drifted on till his son looked into the matter. It was one of my minor jobs to look after the Canteen accounts and pay its bills, and every month when the tradesmen's bills came in I used to feel ashamed, because there was never enough cash in the bank to meet them. We used to get all the bills together, wonder which we could stall off for another month, and pay perhaps half off each of the others. It was all very undignified, and quite unsuitable to Buckingham Palace.

Somehow word of this state of affairs must have reached the ears of the new King, for one day in July, 1939, he sent down for the Canteen accounts and studied them for several days. Then he sent them back with his personal check for £300 to get us out of trouble. With the check he sent a warning: henceforth the Canteen must pay for itself and be run on business lines, or else it would be shut down. As for the £300, that was a loan which he expected to be repaid when profits were made. We started off again on more sensible lines, and by the end of 1941 had a gross profit of £1,100! The King's loan was repaid, and year after year we showed profits of between £900 and £1,200. But none of the cricket club equipment, the tennis gear, the dancing club, or the staff outings by coach in Scotland—all paid for out of Canteen profits— would be possible had it not been for the kindly interest and help of George VI.

Queen Elizabeth, the Queen Mother, is, like her daughter, a very good dancer. In her days at Buckingham Palace she always asked for some old-fashioned numbers to be included in the program at the staff dance. The Valeta, the Dashing White Sergeant, The St. Bernard Waltz, and many other dances almost forgotten today, were among those which she liked to see danced and to dance herself. With her encouragement a dancing school was set up at Buckingham Palace, and some of the Scots girls who had learned the Scots dances at home taught their London friends and colleagues the steps from across the Border, much to the delight of the Queen Mother.

Ever since the days of Queen Victoria and her famous

manservant, John Brown, who was her constant companion in the last years of her life, there has been a closer relationship between members of the Royal Family and their servants north of the Border than seems to be the case in England. The staff social club balls at Buckingham Palace and Windsor Castle derive, I think, really from the ghillies balls at Balmoral, but they differ from these older institutions because at the staff balls the Sovereign, though it is in his or her house that the function is held, comes as the invited guest of the staff. At the more famous ghillies balls at Balmoral the ghillies, their wives, the keepers and workers on the Royal estates, and their wives, are the guests of the Sovereign. The ghillies balls take place in the big ballroom at Balmoral Castle, which is underground. It has an imposing staircase entrance with a kind of platform at the top and a double staircase coming down into the ballroom floor. Opposite is a minstrel's gallery where the band plays.

For the ghillies balls a band is brought in from Kincardine under the direction of a wise lady Mrs. O'Neil, and of course on this occasion most of the dancing is in the Scottish manner, though foxtrots, tangos, waltzes, and even rhumbas are included in the program. Usually there are between 300 and 350 guests, all of them from the estate, and the Queen and members of her house party and the officials of the Royal Household come down and join in the fun.

Dancing starts at nine-thirty and goes on until about eleven-thirty, when usually the Royal Family leave the ballroom with their guests to take refreshments from a buffet set up in the Castle dining room. The ghillies and their friends and the estate people are looked after in the Steward's Room and Servants' Hall, where there is a plentiful supply of sandwiches, cakes, biscuits, pies, cold meats, whisky, port, and beer. Then, after half an hour or an hour's interval, dancing is resumed, but the Royal Family do not come back into the ballroom. They know very well that the staff and estate people will enjoy themselves in a much more hilarious manner in their absence. Then dancing goes on till two-thirty or three in the morning, or even later.

I well remember the first ghillies ball I attended in 1935. It was the first occasion on which I danced with a Royal lady. There was a Paul Jones on the program, and as the band stopped and we all halted to take our partners from the ladies standing opposite, my heart almost stopped when I found that I was standing facing the beautiful Duchess of York, our present Queen Mother. She is a very charming, graceful dancer, and with her wonderful tact and gift of always having the right words to say to put a person at ease, she made me feel unembarrassed at once. We made our progress round the floor in quite a normal manner, and I do not think I have ever enjoyed a dance quite as much. In those days Queen Mary was an amazingly energetic figure at these dances. She loved all Highland dances and many of the old English country dances, which she always had included in the program. She would take part in every one throughout the first half of the dance. But King George V was no great dancer. He would go and sit on the Royal dais at the end of the room and watch the dancers with a keen eye, occasionally turning to one of his staff with a shrewd comment.

King George VI enjoyed the ghillies dances much more than his father used to. He would join in all the fun. I remember when the King, having occasion to leave the ballroom, walked—a striking figure in his kilt of Royal Balmoral tartan and his black dress tunic—up the stairs and paused on the platform. During a lull in the music his voice came clearly across the room uttering the famous words of the late Tommy Handley, who was one of King George VI's favorite radio comedians: "I go—I come back." The King laughed loudly as he finished the phrase, and disappeared from the room, to return some ten minutes or so later and rejoin the dancers.

In the first year of the Queen's reign, when she made her first visit to Balmoral as Sovereign, no ghillies ball was held. Many people thought that this meant that Queen Elizabeth II was breaking with tradition and would hold no more ghillies balls. This was far from the truth. It has always been a rule that in any year the Court goes into mourning no ghillies ball is held when the Sovereign is in residence at Balmoral. So the fact that there was no ghillies ball at Balmoral in 1952 simply meant that the new Queen was still observing mourning for her father.

The staff balls at Sandringham are not so well known as those at Balmoral. At Sandringham there is a very beautifully equipped staff recreation room which was opened by King George V and Queen Mary in 1935 during their Jubilee celebrations. The King paid for the whole of the room—which has a well-sprung dance floor, a concert platform, central heating, and many other amenities—as a tribute, he said at the time, to the "men and women who have served me so well throughout my reign." King George opened the room with a silver-gilt key and held the door open for Queen Mary, I remember. As they toured the hall Queen Mary noticed a dart board. "I would like to try my hand," she said. She was handed six darts, which she threw with some skill at the board, registering a hit with each of them, though she did not score a "double." These Sandringham staff balls are held on New Year's Eve each year, but the Royal Family do not usually attend them, having their own New Year's Eve party at Sandringham House itself.

CHAPTER SEVEN

Balmoral Days and Tales

Looking back on my years in the Royal service, it is Balmoral Castle, that Royal home in the Highlands which the Queen prefers to any of her other residences, that forms the background to my happiest and most intimate memories of the Royal Family.

Away from London much of the stately formality of Court life is dispensed with and the Queen and the Duke of Edinburgh seem much more like ordinary folk and more approachable. The one exception to this is when the Court is at Windsor, where etiquette and protocol are just as closely observed as at Buckingham Palace itself. Perhaps this is because it is so near London. At Balmoral there is the friendliest atmosphere of any of the Royal homes. Here the staff are all on much easier terms with members of the Royal Family than anywhere else. I do not mean that there is anything approaching familiarity, or any lack of respect in the slightest degree, but somehow the Queen and her family always were easier to talk to, more understanding of difficulties, amid the romantic background of Balmoral. This is probably because, on their Highland holiday, they have less pressure on their time and are able to take a closer interest in the lives and activities of those who serve them. In any case, it was at Balmoral that I had more long talks with more members of the Royal Family than I ever did at the Palace, Windsor Castle, or Sandringham.

It was at Balmoral that I first talked to King George V. The circumstances were romantic, because in that summer of 1934 the beautiful Princess Marina of Greece had come to meet the family of her fiancé, Prince George, the Duke of Kent. I shall never forget that day. I had seen the young lovers once or twice in the distance walking along the path in the Castle grounds leading down to the side of the Dee which runs along the boundary of the Balmoral estate. Now I was to meet them face to face.

One morning I was looking through my papers, checking items on a grocer's bill from Aberdeen, when the internal telephone rang. It was the Master of the Household, Sir Derek Keppel, a real courtier of the old school, tall and immaculately dressed, with a carefully trimmed and waxed white mustache. He wanted me to take him the key to the game larder, a big room in one of the outbuildings, kept always at just below freezing point, where the carcasses of stags were—and still are—hung after a stalk, and grouse and other game kept after the shooting parties have returned. I made my way past the kitchens and the coffee room to the room Sir Derek used as his office.

"Have you got the key?" asked Sir Derek in his quiet, cultured voice.

Rather surprised, and conscious that there were several people gathered behind me now in the corridor, I said, "Of course, sir," and proffered him the key.

"No, thank you," said Sir Derek. "I want you to open the larder for the King. He wants to see the stags he shot yesterday."

I turned to go out of the room in a daze, and a few moments later found myself walking along the winding path that leads to the game larder with the King of England on my right and the late Archbishop of Canterbury, Dr. Cosmo (later Lord) Lang, on my left.

It seemed to me I must be dreaming. I know I was blushing when the King spoke to me first, and for the life of me I cannot remember what he said. But with that typical kindliness which his abrupt way of speaking hid, he soon put me at my ease, and I was chatting about the high wind which had sprung up during that morning.

"Yes, indeed, sir," said the Archbishop. "It's a nuisance. I can scarcely keep my wretched hat on."

Behind us walked Queen Mary, with her inevitable parasol. She was in an unusually gay mood, talking to Prince and Princess Nicholas of Greece, the father and mother of Princess Marina. Lagging behind were Prince George and Princess Marina. Their hands were clasped, and it was plain for everyone to see that they were deeply in love. Today, the widowed Duchess of Kent is still, in my humble opinion, a very beautiful woman, and one of the most elegant figures to be seen at a State dinner or Court ball at Buckingham Palace. On that day, twenty years ago, still in the flush of youth, with the heightened radiance of a young girl in love, I thought she was the most beautiful woman I had ever seen.

I fumbled a little, conscious of the King's eye on me, as I opened the heavy wooden, green-painted door of the big larder. The King walked in, followed by the Queen and the rest of the party. Hanging by their hind legs on a butcher's rail were the three fine stags which had fallen to the King's unerring rifle the day before. They had been cleaned, skinned, and dressed, but the heads and antlers were still on the carcasses. They were three magnificent beasts, each weighing between fourteen and eighteen stones. If there was one thing that King George V took real, and justifiable, pride in, it was his shooting, both with a twelve-bore shotgun and a sporting rifle. It was claimed that he was "one of the best shots in Britain." In the Household we knew better. No one who had seen him in action in the grouse butts or on the mountain-side, as we often did, could have any doubt. He was *the* best shot in the country.

For a few seconds the King stood admiring his stags. As always in the Highlands, he wore a Scots-style coat with a kilt of Hunting Stewart tartan, a flat, black Balmoral cap on his head. He always walked with a crummock—the tall stick with a crook handle which Highland shepherds used to guide their sheep. Prodding the carcasses expertly with his crummock, the King said in a gruff and proud voice, and with obvious satisfaction, "There, that's the place to shoot them." He pointed out to the somewhat bewildered Greek Prince and Princess the bullet marks, in each case just beneath the left shoulder. When we had walked back to the Castle, the King thanked me before turning away with the Queen and their guests. For the rest of that day I was a very proud man, and seemed to be walking on air.

Many times since, I talked with King George V, and with his two sons and granddaughter who succeeded him, but never have I felt quite the same touch of exaltation that came to me then. Of course as the years went by I grew more familiar with Royalty. But it was more than that. The peculiar aura of majesty seemed more deeply vested in King George V than in any of his successors, or indeed in any of the many foreign Sovereigns I have met.

Stag-shooting, of course, is still today the central feature around which the life of Balmoral revolves in the months of September and October, when the Royal Family are in residence on Deeside. The Queen follows the rule of her mother and grandmother, that Royal ladies do not join in the shooting on the moors for grouse. Again, like her mother before her, the Queen has made several stalking expeditions in the hills around Balmoral and has brought down a number of fine stags. But though she enjoys the hill-climbing and the long, arduous walks in the bracing Highland air, and the lovely views across the wild countryside that reward the patient stalker, she does not show any real keenness for what is, after all, purely a man's sport.

The routine for the shooting parties has changed very little in the past twenty years. The moors around Balmoral are what the shooters call "late," which means that the grouse hatch out there a few days later than in other parts of the country, so, though the official date for the opening of the grouse season is the "Glorious Twelfth" of August, the Balmoral guns never go out before the fourteenth or fifteenth, though the Royal Family is usually in residence a good ten days before that. This gives the Queen and the Duke of Edinburgh a chance to go over the moors with the head keeper and his men to discuss the season's prospects on the spot. The bigger the grouse population, the bigger the house party in the Castle, was the rule laid down by King George V, and followed to this day. The more grouse that can be taken off the moors, the better. Seven or eight guns is the usual number at Balmoral.

A typical day on the moors starts with a very informal breakfast, at which the men help themselves from hot dishes on the sideboard, before climbing into a big shooting brake which takes them to the nearest point to the butts. One of the many improvements which the Queen has introduced on her Scottish estates is an extension of the existing road so that the brakes can get much closer to some of the distant moors, thus cutting out a long walk back. The brake with the guns is followed by another in which are the "gentlemen's gentlemen" who are to act as loaders—all in tweeds and gray flannels, or the kilt, like their masters. King George VI always asked his police officer, Chief Superintendent Hugh Cameron, C.V.O., now retired, to act as his loader, and a faster, more certain worker in the butts I have never seen. To have a good loader is half the battle for a crack shot who wants to make a good bag. Cameron, devoted to his Royal charge, used to enjoy a day on the moors almost as much as the King did. With the loaders go the actual guns, the cartridges, and the dogs. They leave about 9 A.M., and drive off to one of the several moors—Torbeg, Micros, Delnabo, or Corndavon—which border the estates. On most days the ladies of the house party drive out about noon to join the guns for a shooting lunch.

Early in the morning estate workers put up a big tent at a chosen spot on the moors and here the Royal Chef, Mr. Ronnie Aubrey, sends his food, china, and cutlery. It is a major operation conveying to the tent the piles of soup and luncheon plates and other china, stacked in tens or eights, and neatly tied up in linen napkins to protect them from damage over the rough roads, together with the glasses, cutlery, and other table appointments. For Royal meals everything must be exactly right, even if it is only a picnic.

From two or three big hampers the Chef unpacks the foodstuffs. In prewar days the almost invariable menu was: Scotch broth, cold game pie, small mutton pies (each making about two mouthfuls), stuffed rolls filled with chopped chicken and ham dressed with homemade mayonnaise, finger portions of shooting pudding (a huge Christmas pudding mixture made with two or three gallons of very old ale), with apples, pears, or plums to follow. Today a supply of fresh raspberries and cream—one of the Queen's favorite dessert dishes—is often included.

The small mutton pies are made from a recipe worked out by one of Queen Victoria's chefs well over a hundred years ago, and unchanged to the present day. These pies were always served at the evening Courts of prewar days and are still provided at balls and late parties at Buckingham Palace in these days. While meat was still rationed after the war, and mutton could not be used, Queen Elizabeth, the present Queen Mother, suggested substituting venison, of which naturally there is always a plentiful supply from the Balmoral and Windsor stags. Her idea was a brilliant success, and venison is still used as an alternative to mutton today. Standing in the butts can be chilling work in the cold wind, and whisky, sherry, and port are always available at the shooting lunches, with cherry brandy as a liqueur for the ladies.

In the days of King George V and up to the start of the war in 1939, serving this lunch was an elaborate ritual. The footmen were driven out from the Castle wearing a special all-black livery and black bowler hats, with the King's Steward, Mr. Ainslie, to supervise them. By a tradition started by Albert, the Prince Consort, and maintained up to 1939, the Steward while at Balmoral wears a unique livery, consisting of a coat cut with tails as for morning dress, single-breasted waistcoat, and trousers without turn-ups, all cut in black-and-white shepherds' plaid tweed. Strange as this garb may be, it looks in fact ideal against the quiet gray-and-mauve background of the distant hills. After the luncheon interval the guns go back to the butts, moving to a different part of the moor, and shooting continues until the light begins to fail around 4 or 4:30 P.M. The ladies retire to the Castle after lunch to spend the afternoon in the garden, or in driving to one of the many beauty spots, like the Braes o' Mar—one of the Queen Mother's special favorites—which abound in the neighborhood of the Royal estate. A shooting tea—a simple meal of paste and jam sandwiches, with plain currant and Chelsea buns—is served in the tent before the guns leave to return to the Castle at about 5:30 P.M.

After taking their baths and changing into Highland dress or dinner jackets, the men come down to sit with the ladies in the drawing room, taking a glass of sherry or a cocktail as they talk over the day's sport and plan that for the following day.

Both King George V and his son George VI were tremendously keen on keeping accurate records of all game shot at Balmoral, Sandringham, and Windsor. It was one of my jobs in the evening to write out a game card for the King and one for each guest who had been in the day's shooting party. These cards are in the form of a small, white booklet stamped with the Royal Arms. On the front cover I would write the date and the name of the gun: H.M. The King, The Duke of . . ., The Earl of . . ., and so on. Inside I wrote the name of the beat, and the names in correct order of precedence (a matter about which both King Georges were, and the present Queen is, insistent on absolute accuracy). On the other side of the card I recorded the day's bag, worked out from the returns which the keepers brought me, noting the number of young grouse shot, then the number of old grouse, followed by pheasant, partridges, and any other game, like pigeons, capercaillies, snipe, hare, or rabbit.

All these figures and names must also be entered after each day's shoot in the big, red, leather-bound Game Book as a permanent record. These books go back without a break to the year 1910, when King George V first shot at Balmoral. I well remember one occasion when King George VI found a mistake in the shooting cards. He had a very remarkable memory for figures. And when he was convinced he was right it took a lot of courage to contradict him, and needed unassailable facts to persuade him that he was wrong. This night my telephone rang ten minutes after I had sent the King's card up to him.

"The King wants you at once," came the voice of the Page, Mr. Freddie Smith.

Wondering what could be wrong, I went up to the King's business room. He was sitting at his desk, pencil in hand, head down, studying the card and obviously puzzled.

"It's all wrong, Corbitt," he said without preliminaries. "How did you get these figures?"

I told the King they had been brought me by the servant in charge of the game larder.

"Then he missed two brace of grouse," said the King. "Find out why."

The King used to keep a record of the grouse sent out as presents to friends, the number of birds issued to the Chef for use in the Castle kitchens, and the number left in stock. In the game larder I found the ghillie responsible and told him the King was demanding a recount. When I got back the King was sipping the whisky-and-soda which he always took about 6:15 P.M. I told him that our check gave the same results. At this he looked displeased. Putting down his glass, he told me to go and see the headkeeper and ask him what had gone wrong. This mission was a failure. The dour Scots keeper, Alexander Gillan, would not budge. All the birds shot that day had been brought in.

"You can go and tell the King that, laddie," he said.

I did.

"You're all wrong downstairs," the King rejoined a little testily. "You can't count."

Now it was my turn to get cross, and I told the King it wasn't my fault. Then as I looked at him, with the muscles of his cheeks twitching, as they did whenever he was annoyed, I had an idea.

"Has Your Majesty asked the Duke of Gloucester if he has taken any of today's birds to Birkhall?" I asked.

The King lifted his telephone and asked for the Duke. Yes, the Duke told him, he had taken a couple of brace. Then I heard the King tell his brother Harry in no uncertain manner that he must never take birds away again without telling him. This was a small thing, but illustrates the accuracy of King George's memory, which I can never recall being at fault.

The Duke of Gloucester, himself a fine shot, and his Duchess, Scots by birth, always enjoyed their visits to Balmoral, where they used to stay at Birkhall, the dower house a few miles away, which King George VI and Queen Elizabeth occupied as Duke and Duchess of York, and where the Queen spent her Scottish holidays for the first ten years of her life. In the war, however, the Castle house parties were smaller, and the Gloucesters stayed with the King and Queen in the Castle.

It was during one of these visits that the Duchess, whom I always think of as one of the most charming people in all the Royal Family, made a gesture to my wife (who, as her contribution to the war effort, worked long hours in the office with me as my assistant) and me which was typical of her kindly, thoughtful nature. Some months before, I had been asked, at the Duchess's request, to talk to her housekeeper in London, at the big flat in Curzon Street, Mayfair, which the King put at their disposal while York House, their home in St. James's Palace, was uninhabitable. This flat, in fact, was the "first emergency" home for the King and Queen should the Palace be rendered uninhabitable; but never, fortunately, did it have to be used for that purpose. In the big drawing room, the housekeeper told me that her Royal mistress was very concerned about her small son, Prince Richard, who, she thought, was not getting quite the right kind of food. In London and at Northampton, where the Gloucesters have their country home, it was unobtainable. Could I procure some for the young Prince? I was able to obtain the desired items of diet, and the Duke of Gloucester used to take them home with him from time to time when he went to Northampton for the weekend.

When the Gloucesters, complete with the small Prince and his nanny, Miss Lightbody—now in charge of the Royal nursery for Prince Charles and Princess Anne—arrived at Balmoral a few months later, Miss Lightbody came down to my office one morning with an invitation from the Duchess for my wife and myself to go up and see the Prince at six o'clock that evening. Up we went, and there, standing at the nursery door with that charming half-smile on her face, was the Duchess, waiting to greet us. She is very attractive, with freckles on her nose which do not show in her photographs. Her young son was at her side, looking very bonny and fit. His mother told him to shake hands with us, which he did with such grave dignity that it was as much as we could do to keep from laughing. "Off you go now, Richard," said the Duchess, and the Prince hurried away into his nursery. Then the Duchess shook hands with us both, and told us how glad and grateful she had been for the regular weekly sugar supplies. She thanked us both warmly and told us, "I wanted you to see for yourselves how well and strong the young Prince is, due, of course, to your help," and added that she would not have felt happy if she had left Balmoral without our seeing the Prince.

It gave both of us real pleasure to know that the Duchess had thought of us in this delightful fashion. Nor was that the end of the story. Four months later, back at Buckingham

Palace, just before Christmas, an orderly came in and handed me a large envelope embossed with a capital "H" (for Henry) and a coronet. In it I found a fine, family photograph of the Gloucesters, signed at the bottom, "Henry and Alice." It remains one of my most valued Palace souvenirs.

Deerstalking, the other great Balmoral interest, is, of course, an individual sport. In the old days the King or any one of the guests would go out with one of the ghillies who had marked down a stag for killing, at the time when the grouse season was drawing to a close. The stalker and the ghillie drive out about 10 A.M. to some wild and bleak spot in the mountains, whence they set off on foot to track down the stag. No organized luncheons can be provided on this grueling expedition. Instead there is a pie or two and some sandwiches in a haversack carried by the ghillie. In this haversack, too, is a flask, with a measure of whisky, and the Balmoral saying is, by the whisky hangs the stag. That is to say that any guest who sees to it that there is sufficient whisky for the ghillie as well as for himself on the hillside will come back with a stag. True or false as this may be, I know that several guests who neglected this precaution (perhaps by bad luck) have returned empty-handed.

One of the most wonderful sights at Balmoral is to watch the stags being brought in from the mountainside by the hill ponies. The huge bulk of the dead stag dwarfs the tiny ponies till you think they must fall. But they are sure-footed and strong. Meat from the stags is used both for the Royal table and for the other messes in the Household. Members of the Royal Family greatly enjoy roast haunch of venison, and it always amused me to hear complaints from the senior servants in the Steward's Room and their juniors in the Servants' Hall, especially during wartime, when we often served roast or stewed venison to them. What was good enough for the King and Queen did not always suit their palate!

King George VI, always fond of country walking, was an enthusiastic deerstalker right up to the time in 1948 when his leg began to trouble him. Even then he refused to be beaten and attempted to go stalking by car. The last time he tried for a stag was at the end of what proved to be his last visit to Balmoral in 1951. He was very ill indeed throughout this trip. I recall spending twenty minutes in his study about the middle of the stay when he was complaining that the grouse that year were not up to standard—in fact nothing seemed to be right.

I can see him now, wearing a green tweed stalking suit and looking very tired and thin.

"I can no longer shoot as I used to do," he told me. It was then, I think, that I realized he was a dying man.

Just before he was flown down to London for the X-ray examination which revealed that he was suffering from lung trouble, he slipped away after tea one day for an hour or two's stalking. The head stalker, McHardy, was determined that this time his Royal master should get a stag.

A strange thing about stags, which I had learned many years before from an experienced stalker, is that while a car is moving slowly across the moor, a stag will remain motionless watching you all the time, but if you stop he immediately senses danger and gallops away.

The stalker had marked a fine beast, and led the King's shooting brake close up to the place where the stag was grazing. The beast was now in rifle range, with the brake crawling at snail's pace. The ghillie got out while the brake was still moving, followed by the King and the only other occupant, besides the chauffeur—the King's detective. McHardy stooped, arching his back to make a gun rest for the King, who took careful aim at the motionless stag outlined in the distance, on high ground against the evening sky. Just as the King had the beast well in his rifle sight, the air was rent by the sound of a motor horn. That was enough for the stag, which disappeared before the King had any chance of a shot.

The King, I was told that evening by the detective, rated the unfortunate chauffeur in a very decided manner. What had happened was that the Royal driver had leaned forward with his arm across the steering wheel and inadvertently touched the button.

King George disliked being disturbed or interrupted at table. I can recall only two occasions on which I saw him get up with his guests in the middle of a meal. One was when he heard the tragic news of his brother's death in the air crash, the other was also at Balmoral, where one evening, just as the second course of the dinner was ready to be taken from the kitchen to the table, the air was rent with the wailing of the special Castle air-raid siren, meaning that enemy planes were in the vicinity, and that everyone must take cover at once. I hurriedly left my office and ran into the courtyard. Here I found some of the Royal ghillies who were on the Castle A.R.P. staff looking strangely unfamiliar in their anti-gas capes and steel helmets. It was the first time they had had to act on the "real thing," and they put every ounce of their energies into it, dashing about with stirrup pumps and buckets of sand, determined to save the Royal Family and the Castle, come what might. To us, from London, to whom the sound of the sirens had been a familiar, if hated, companion for so long, there was something comic about the frantic excitement of the Highlanders.

The Castle Steward had ordered the footmen to their pre-arranged positions on the Castle tower, where they were to act as roof spotters. Obediently, they had abandoned their carrying trays in the kitchen to rush up to their action stations. But there seemed no sign of aircraft, and I made my way back into the Castle to find the kitchen empty save for the white-clad figure of the Chef. He stood in the doorway, demanding to know where everybody had gone and what was to happen to his dinner. He saw no reason why a German bomber or two should be allowed to spoil his carefully prepared dishes.

The King and Queen with half a dozen of their guests had been conducted down to their shelter, deep beneath the Castle foundations, when, with the Chef still loudly bemoaning the fate of his dinner, the welcome sound of the "All Clear" was heard. The King and Queen and their guests returned to the dining room, the footmen, hastily removing their steel helmets, hurried down the stairs to pick up their trays again—and dinner was resumed, the second course, a casserole of grouse, being taken to the table twenty minutes late, and, according the Chef, completely ruined. Ruined or not, the dish was greatly enjoyed by the Royal couple and their guests, and the King, to everyone's surprise, treated the matter as a joke, roaring with laughter, instead of getting into a temper, as we had expected. He laughed even more loudly when he heard from the telephone switchboard operator the cause of all the bother. It was a solitary German plane picked up by our observers well out over the North Sea, heading apparently for the Aberdeenshire coast. It turned back before encountering our coastal defenses, but the loyal Scots, knowing that their King was in their midst, were taking no chances, and set the alarm system in motion at once.

One of my last memories, and a mournful one at that, of King George VI was at Balmoral in August, 1951, his last visit there. He sent for me to his study to talk about the grouse, complaining that this year the birds all seemed small and most difficult to shoot. Then he commented on the mousse of grouse which had been served at lunch the day before. "It was very good indeed; I enjoyed it," said the King, adding with a smile, "Try some yourself, Corbitt, and see if I am not right."

I was shocked at the change which had come over the King in a few days. He looked dispirited and exhausted, so much so that I began to wonder if he would ever see Balmoral again. As if reading my thoughts, he got up and walked to the window, looking out at the Cairngorm Mountains he knew and loved so well.

"I don't seem to be able to shoot nearly as well nowadays as I used to," he said, half to himself. "Perhaps it's my fault; not the size of the birds." It was indeed sad to hear him talk like this.

CHAPTER EIGHT

When Royalty Celebrates
Christmases and Birthdays

A REGULAR timetable, arrangements planned well ahead, a diary almost unvarying from year to year—these were features of the Royal life under King George V, and also under King George VI, except during the war years, when no one high or low could plan in advance. Queen Elizabeth II does not run her life on quite the same rigid lines, but nonetheless the Royal year is fairly well mapped out in advance.

The most regular feature of the Royal year, unchanged in any of the last four or five reigns, is the family Christmas party at Sandringham. Family festivities hold a high place in the Royal regard, though birthdays, strangely enough, are allowed to pass with but little ceremony. This is because the birthdays of all members of the Royal Family, except for the Sovereign, are treated purely as private occasions, and the parties are therefore small and confined to members of the family and intimate friends. Nor, contrary to public belief, are Royal birthdays made the occasion for romantic announcements, as witness the fiasco, from the Press' point of view, on Princess Margaret's twenty-first birthday at Balmoral Castle in 1951.

Fleet Street had decided, for reasons best known to itself,

that the announcement of the Princess's engagement was to be made on this day, so a large number of reporters and photographers descended on Deeside, filling all the hotels and asking questions from everyone they could find. There was the usual small dinner party and dance at Balmoral Castle, attended by a number of the Princess's young friends—but no announcement was forthcoming. We in the Castle smiled, for we had known that whatever the outcome of the Princess's friendship with Group Captain Peter Townsend, it was certain that no announcement of her engagement could possibly be made on her twenty-first birthday.

The birthday of the Sovereign, however, falls into a different category. It is honored by the ceremony of Trooping the Color by the Brigade of Guards on the Horse Guards Parade: the King or Queen rides over from Buckingham Palace to Horse Guards Parade to inspect the line of scarlet-clad Guardsmen and then to take the salute as they march past, afterward riding back at the head of the Foot Guards to Buckingham Palace, where he or she takes the salute on horseback in front of the center gates of the Palace while the Guards go marching by.

I have seen this ceremony many times and have never failed to be stirred by the martial pageantry of what must be the most perfectly performed and executed military ceremonial in the world today.

Because of this time-old ceremony, and because it is traditional for a list of Honors, known as the Birthday Honors, to be issued each year to commemorate the Sovereign's anniversary, the birthday of the reigning Monarch is always observed on the second Thursday in June, and not on the actual day of the birth anniversary. In the case of King George VI the actual birthday was December 14. The Queen's birthday is April 21. Neither of these dates would be suitable, for a variety of reasons, for the official celebrations. King George VI's birthday was much too near to the New Year Honors for the issue of an Honors list, nor would the weather have been sufficiently reliable to plan a ceremony like the Trooping of the Color. Much the same considerations, particularly the latter, apply to the April birthday of the present Queen.

Sandringham is, I think, the pleasantest and most homely of all the Royal residences. It is here that the Royal Christmas is celebrated every year, and the spirit of the old-fashioned Christmas is fully maintained. This red brick house, bought by Edward VII when he was Prince of Wales, was converted into a real home for members of the Royal Family. Several of them, including King George V and King George VI, were born here; several, including both these Monarchs, died in this most English of country homes.

I remember when I first went to the Royal home in Norfolk for Christmas being staggered at the size and variety of the King's Christmas present list—and, of course, it was only with the Household staff and tenants' lists that I was concerned. The private presents of members of the Royal Family to one another, and those from the King and Queen, were outside my ken. Yet the ones I did have to deal with constituted a really remarkable total running into several hundreds of pounds. Today, despite the contraction in almost every direction of Royal expenditure, the list which the Queen approves is very little smaller than that of her grandfather's day. This is the one thing on which the Queen, like her father before her, has taken a firm stand, and will allow no cutting down. The Royal bounty at Christmas is as generous to the servants, staff, tenants, and officials as ever it was.

The Royal gifts are spread over a number of various lists, for different categories of people. For example, four hundred names of the aged poor in the Royal Borough of Windsor are on the list. Each of these people, men and women alike, used to receive one hundredweight of coal as a personal gift from the King. When coal was rationed during the war this custom, of course, had to be given up. Gifts of money were sent instead to each of the Windsor poor on the list, compiled, by the way, by the incumbents of the local parishes. Another separate list has on it the names of every policeman on duty at Buckingham Palace. Each of these used to receive in prewar days a turkey or a goose, whichever they preferred, with a pound of prime pork sausages to go with the bird as a Christmas gift from the King. This custom, too, had to be suspended during the war, and has, alas, not been renewed. Cash gifts, in the form of savings certificates, make a poor substitute, in my opinion, for the more personal touch of the Christmas-dinner gift.

Gifts of food went in prewar days to the servants at the Palace, at Windsor Castle, at Balmoral, and at Sandringham in the form of a two-pound Christmas pudding and a large mince pie for every man and woman. This particular custom was revived soon after the war by King George VI, and continues to this day, but the puddings and pies, which when I first went to the Palace were made by the King's Chef from an old Royal Family recipe, are today bought ready-made from one of the big provision firms, which, considering that there are something over nine hundred recipients to be thought of, is not perhaps surprising! This Royal gift list includes the station masters at Euston, Liverpool Street, Wolferton (for Sandringham), and Ballater (for Balmoral), the stations which the Royal Family use regularly during the year, and a number of pensioned-off old servants, and other former members of the staff.

As Christmas draws near, the same spirit of excitement

that pervades every house in the land also pervades Buckingham Palace. A few days before Christmas, the Queen and her family drive off to King's Cross to board the Royal train for Sandringham. (Few people, incidentally, know why the Sovereign always leaves from King's Cross, and not Liverpool Street, on these journeys to Norfolk. Traffic density around the Bank is only a secondary reason. The real reason is to avoid the City of London, where the Lord Mayor has the traditional and historic right to greet the Sovereign whenever he or she crosses the City boundaries. To do this at Christmas time, with all the attendant ceremonial, would add considerably to traffic delays, and spoil the holiday character of the journey.)

Buckingham Palace is officially "closed" until the Court returns to London, usually some time in early February. This means that only a skeleton staff is kept on duty with a few officials coming in every day to attend to the Queen's business. It is a tradition in the Royal Household that there shall be fair play and equal shares for all, so, for the benefit of those not traveling to Sandringham, there is a special Christmas dinner in advance served the day before the Court leaves, with roast turkey, plum pudding, whisky, beer, and port, for everyone in the house. Every member of the Household, officials and servants included, is received by the Queen and the Duke of Edinburgh over Christmastide, those not going to Sandringham at the Palace before she leaves, the rest at Sandringham after she has made her broadcast on Christmas Day.

It was on one of these occasions—Christmas, 1952—that I had my last talk with the Queen. This time I went with the Palace contingent, though I was, in fact, leaving for Sandringham that evening. The Queen received us individually in the Forty-Four Room (so called because of the date, 1844, which was embossed on the ceiling when it was redecorated for Queen Victoria), to give us each a Christmas present. When I walked in, she was standing alone by a long trestle table, covered with a red velvet cloth and laden with parcels. The Queen greeted me with a warm smile and put out her hand for me to shake.

"Are you coming to Sandringham this time?" she asked, and I said I would be there to make arrangements for supplies, and to tend to staff accommodation, with the help of the Sandringham housekeeper, Miss Jessie Robertson.

"Will your family be going down too?" asked the Queen, to which I replied that they would indeed.

"How old is your boy now?" was the next question, to which I answered, "He's seven, Your Majesty." So, for several minutes the conversation went on, with the Queen asking me in the most friendly way whether we were comfortable at home, whether we had a house or a flat, and a score of other human questions. At last she asked, "Has your boy a room of his own?" and when I told her he had, she said with a smile (for she had already made inquiries and knew in advance), "Then this will, perhaps, do for his bed." With that, the Queen handed me a fine gold-colored eiderdown as my Christmas gift. It was bulky and somewhat difficult to carry, and as I tucked it under my arm so that I could make a dignified exit, the Queen began to laugh and I joined in, and for a fleeting moment Royal dignity and ceremony were forgotten. That talk which I can recall word for word today was typical of the kindliness of the Queen, always full of thought for others, deeply and genuinely interested in the welfare, family life, and comfort of all those who serve her, just as her mother was before her, and still is today.

I remember a similar talk with Queen Elizabeth at Sandringham in December, 1939; I had married a few months before, and the Queen knew all about this, as she made it her business to know about the domestic affairs of all the King's staff. On that occasion my present was a lovely striking clock, and I remember Queen Elizabeth telling me she had heard of my marriage. "Where are you living now?" she asked, and, after a few more questions, gave me the clock with the words, "I do hope you will find this useful in your home."

In the ballroom at Sandringham on Christmas Eve a large Christmas tree, perhaps eighteen feet high, is placed in a corner. It is always a tree cut from the Sandringham woods by the Royal foresters and brought in by them a day or two in advance. I have often seen King George V and Queen Mary, and King George VI and Queen Elizabeth, busy in the ballroom in the early afternoon of Christmas Eve, going through piles of presents on a table near the Christmas tree arranging for a little label to be tied on each gift for their friends, the guests in the house party, and members of the Household. The tree is always lit with colored fairy lights, and King George VI and Queen Elizabeth used to take great delight in hanging the little presents and parcels upon it, helped in latter years by Princess Elizabeth and Princess Margaret.

It was always at four o'clock precisely that King George V would walk round the house and across the grounds to the stables. There, in the open air, he would take part in a ceremony in which he acted as the Squire of Sandringham which always delighted him. He would present large cuts of prime Sandringham home-killed beef to each worker on his estate. The joints were laid out on a long wooden table, and the portions given to each person were generous in weight—perhaps six or seven pounds at a minimum. This was always known as the King's Beef, and great trouble was always taken at the Sandringham farm to ensure that only the finest beef was supplied. At 6:30 P.M. on Christmas Eve the local carol singers always come to Sandringham House, stand outside, and sing their carols through the open door.

It was Queen Elizabeth, the Queen Mother, who introduced a new feature of carol-singing into the Royal Christmas festivities. Before the Court left Buckingham Palace, the boys of the choir from the Chapel Royal, at St. James's Palace, would come across to Buckingham Palace with their choir-master and the Sub-Dean of the Chapel Royal to sing a pro-gram of Christmas hymns and carols to the King and Queen, the Princesses, and any other members of the Royal Family who happened to be in London. I was always able to listen to this lovely Christmas concert. After the concert King George VI used to hand each one of the choir making his first visit to Buckingham Palace a Bible inscribed with a message of good wishes and the King's signature.

At Sandringham on Christmas morning the Royal Family always walk across the park to the little church of St. Mary Magdalene. In latter years so many thousands of motorists have gathered round the church, and attempted to get in to attend Divine Service with the Royal Family, that drastic measures had to be taken. The King told the Rector of San-dringham not to allow any except regular parishioners into the church on Christmas morning. The others, coming from many miles, perhaps, to attend the service, however, could not be ignored, so that the King readily consented to an idea sug-gested by the former Rector, the Reverend J. Anderson, that the service should be relayed to the crowds outside through loud-speakers. This has been done in the last few years, and members of the church congregation have collected money from the visitors for the church funds.

After church the Royal Family walk back to Sandringham House for luncheon, which is always served at 1:15 P.M. Here is the very essence of Christmas. On the sideboard is a boar's head, gleaming with glaze, complete with eyes and tusks, stuffed with special forcemeat and truffles and mounted on a large silver dish. Around this are grouped cold meats—ham, tongue, beef, and so on—and on the sideboard is a variety of nuts, figs, dates, muscatels, almonds, and other good things.

The menu is always the same: a simple one of soup, followed by roast turkey with chippolata sausages, the appropriate vegetables, and afterward Christmas pudding and mince pies. In the days of King George V the menu was always written in French, it still is today.

After lunch comes the Royal Christmas talk, which was started by King George V, and at first dreaded and afterward loved by King George VI, and now given by Queen Elizabeth II—the annual heart-to-heart fireside talk over the wireless.

Immediately after his broadcast, King George V would rejoin Queen Mary and the other members of their house party in the drawing room, and then go with Queen Mary to a special place adjoining the ballroom. They would stay there for an hour or more, giving presents to every member of their staff as they filed slowly past, shaking hands, and bowing and curtsying to the King and Queen. I remember, as if it were yesterday, receiving my first present on that Christmas Day of 1934. It was a lovely silver pencil in a box, which Queen Mary herself handed to me with the words: "I hope this little present will be useful to you." Royal hopes were indeed fulfilled for I have used it ever since. With pride I had it engraved myself with the words: "From H.M. the Queen, Sandringham, 1934."

One of the many delightful changes that took place when King George VI came to the throne was the special nursery celebrations at Sandringham at Christmas time for Princess Elizabeth and her sister, Princess Margaret. There was a special, small Christmas tree for the children, special crackers for them, and a nursery turkey which weighed from eight to ten pounds. The same sort of thing goes on at Sandringham now for the benefit of Prince Charles, the Duke of Cornwall, and his sister, Princess Anne.

Boxing Day is always a quiet day at Sandringham after the festivities of Christmas. There is a special rule that there shall be no shooting parties on Boxing Day, even though it is then the height of the pheasant- and partridge-shooting season. Instead the guns, led nowadays by the Duke of Edinburgh, go out the day following Boxing Day. The reason for this is the Queen's desire that her estate workers shall have two complete days' holiday, and that the beaters, gamekeepers, and others necessary for the organizing of a pheasant shoot shall not be called on to work on Boxing Day—another typical example of her thoughtfulness and consideration for others.

Much is made in the Royal Family of the New Year. On New Year's Eve, while the staff are dancing in their recreation room, the Royal Family with their guests play card games in the drawing room, as they like to do in the evenings at Sandringham. Just before midnight Pages would bring in refreshments and hand round a drink to everyone of the Royal party and their guests with which to pledge the New Year. Then Queen Elizabeth, the Queen Mother, would send her personal attendant—a tall man with dark hair—outside into the drive, so that he might "first foot" in the ancient tradition of Scotland. The Page would approach the front hall and knock loudly on the big front door, which was immediately opened to him after the hall clock—a lovely grandfather clock which has stood there for many and many a long year—had struck the twelve chimes. The Page was escorted to the drawing room. Entering with a low bow, he would wish the King and Queen, "A happy and prosperous New Year to both Your

Majesties." Then the King would offer the Page a drink, and everyone would toast to Happiness and Prosperity in the New Year.

Many other Scottish customs, such as the bringing in of a piece of coal as a token of good luck, were introduced into the Royal circle by Queen Elizabeth. Very often after the cere-monies at midnight there would be dancing to the music of the radio-gramophone to start the New Year. It was all very happy and informal. But next day there were usually some thick heads among the Royal servants and members of the staff, for dancing in the recreation room always went on until three in the morning, with plentiful refreshments supplied. As a sidelight on the changed conditions between the reigns of George V and George VI, I may add that the refreshments at these staff dances on New Year's Eve are paid for by the staff themselves out of the staff Canteen funds. In the days of King George V refreshments of this kind would have been supplied liberally from the Royal cellars.

Sandringham is a very cozy country house, with everything in it to add to the comfort of the Royal Family and their guests. But in one way it is very old-fashioned. In every room of the big house there is an open fireplace, and wood fires are the order of the day. For weeks before the Royal Family arrive to take up residence for Christmas, the employees in the wood yard and sawing mill on the Royal estate are kept busy cutting up trees from the forests into logs for burning in the house. The logs are carried by porters up to the Royal apartments and the other rooms and stacked in large basket-like containers by the sides of the fireplaces. The servants go round at regular intervals to tend the fires, but King George VI loved to tend his own fire and stacked it carefully with wood, holding (and rightly, I believe) that there is a definite art in the building of a wood fire to give the maximum warmth for the minimum consumption of fuel.

Another holiday festival always celebrated in traditional fashion by the Queen, as it used to be by her father and her grandfather before her, is Easter. It is the Royal tradition that Easter shall be spent at Windsor Castle, where the gardens and grounds are at their best, with masses of daffodils gilding the sloping green lawns and the terraces around the Castle, and the enchanting view of the Thames in the distance. Food at Easter is always simple and the tradition of hot-cross buns is faithfully observed. There is also a large Simnel cake baked for the Royal party and served on the afternoon of Good Friday, and also on Saturday and Easter Sunday, in the drawing room. Easter eggs for the children are another feature of the Royal Easter, and the Duke of Cornwall and Princess Anne have enormous fun chasing round the garden and looking for the eggs that "Daddy" and "Mummy" have hidden (but not too carefully), so that the children shall have a chance to find them. The Queen must often remember as she watches her children running round the gardens, seeking here, there, and everywhere for the eggs they will surely find in a few moments, the days when she herself and her sister, as little girls, did just the same thing in the same place, watched by their father and mother.

On Easter Sunday the Queen always attends Divine Service, either in the Chapel Royal in Windsor Great Park, which stands opposite Royal Lodge, or else in St. George's Chapel itself at Windsor Castle. But wherever she is she asks particularly that her church-going shall be regarded as private, and crowds are discouraged from attending services because she is present. This is not because the Queen wishes to hide herself from her people, but because she believes that her religious devotions should remain her private affair.

At Windsor Castle another old Royal tradition dating back at least to the days of Queen Victoria, if not beyond, is still observed. That is the awakening of the Sovereign by the Royal Pipe-Major. At eight-thirty every morning the Queen's Piper parades on the East Terrace of the Castle, playing martial airs on his pipes, which serve as a sort of alarm clock for the Queen, as they used to for her grandfather and father before her. There is, and has always been, in the Royal Family, a deep love of the pipe music of Scotland. I myself am an admirer of pipe music, and when at Windsor Castle never failed to turn out early in the morning to hear the King's Piper. At Balmoral, of course, the pipers are even more in evidence than they are at Windsor. At dinner the King's Pipers used to play marching round the dining table, and so out into the Castle Hall, where they would all be refreshed with the traditional dram of whisky. The present Queen maintains this, as she does so many of the other traditions set by her father and grandfather before her.

It is at Balmoral Castle, of course, that the Royal Family's love of Scotland and things Scottish finds its greatest manifestation. Most of the rooms at Balmoral Castle are still furnished in the Scottish Victorian manner. This is particularly true of the dining room, a lovely apartment with long windows overlooking the tower of the Castle, and some wonderful pansy beds which lead the eye gently down to the Dee running at the boundary of the Royal estate. The curtains in this room are of heavy Royal Stewart tartan.

At either end of the room are large paintings by Winterhalter, the famous Court painter of Victorian days. One displays the youthful Queen Victoria in all the radiant loveliness of her younger days. The other, naturally, is of the Prince Consort, the architect of Balmoral Castle as it exists today, and the man responsible for the planning of all the interior decorations of the Castle. The detailed mind of Prince Albert can be seen everywhere at Balmoral. Because Balmoral was to be the Scottish home of the Royal Family, everything in it, down to the smallest item of domestic equipment, had to bear the imprint of things Scottish—and so they do even to this day. The traditions laid down by the Prince Consort are still carried on, and no Royal dinner is ever served at Balmoral without its accompaniment of pipe music. There are five Queen's Pipers, led by an ex-Pipe-Major of the Scots Guards. Each evening at dinner the pipers play in the dining room and in the hall, and the program of music is a set affair: a march, then a strathspey, then a reel, and finally a march.

I have seen new visitors to Balmoral, especially those coming from the United States, or even from the south of England, receive quite a shock as the full blast of the pipes struck their ears for the first time. But pipe music is something to which you become accustomed. Particularly fond of the Scottish pipe music was King Edward VIII, now the Duke of Windsor. Indeed, he learned to play the pipes himself, and on one occasion, at least, composed some music for the pipes. That was in 1934, after the Prince of Wales, as he then was, had paid a visit to the island of Majorca. When he came back he composed a lively air for the pipes which he called, "Majorca."

I remember one day up at Balmoral, after playing golf on the private course I was on my way back to the Castle through the driving rain with my companion when we saw the familiar figure of the Prince, wrapped in a heavy Inverness cape, with the pipes across his shoulder, playing away as he marched up and down in the pouring rain. His instructor, Pipe-Major Forsyth, late of the Scots Guards, and Chief Piper to the King, stood watching his Royal pupil a trifle gloomily and getting slowly soaked. Forsyth and his fellow-pipers were all delighted at the great interest in their art shown by the Heir to the Throne, but their delight was considerably tempered when the Prince insisted on marching up and down in the rain and getting everyone soaked as he played his latest composition. Many a time I saw the Prince playing the pipes. He seemed to be quite expert, and I have heard Pipe-Major Forsyth speak highly of his Royal pupil.

The incident of the pipes in the rain was, I have often thought, typical of Edward VIII. If he wanted to do a thing he did it, quite unconscious of the fact that he might possibly be causing discomfort to others. I could not imagine King George VI, or the present Queen, however much they might want to play the pipes, taking their servants out into the rain and getting them wet through.

At Balmoral Castle, though the Royal Family is on private holiday, some State duties still have to be performed by the Sovereign. Notable among these is the annual succession of official guests who come to stay for a weekend or perhaps four days at Balmoral. The Prime Minister of the day is always invited to Balmoral, though sometimes other official commitments prevent his coming, and in that case King George VI used always to excuse his Prime Minister, as I believe the Queen does today, from obeying the Royal Command. But Prime Ministers and members of the Cabinet, Archbishops and Bishops, all are invited to Balmoral, and come in a succession of visits. It is a little-known fact about Balmoral Castle that every Prime Minister who has visited Balmoral, dating from the days of Queen Victoria, has presented a portrait of himself to the Sovereign. There is a special room on the ground floor at Balmoral overlooking the spacious lawn and the fountain which plays during the daytime, known as the Prime Minister's Room, which is always set aside for his use. Every Prime Minister from the beginning of the century until now has slept in this room.

I remember the visit of Mr. Neville Chamberlain during his Premiership. He came late in the season of that fateful year of 1938. Now, the Premier was no hand with a gun, and he craved the King's permission not to go out with the shooting party in the mornings. But Mr. Chamberlain was a very keen fisherman, and the waters of the Dee are a paradise for anglers, with salmon and trout in plenty.

Every morning at 10 A.M. the Prime Minister would walk out of the Castle carrying with him sandwiches, and coffee in a thermos flask. He would select his water for the day and there spend many happy hours. I used to watch him standing there with his waders on, deep in the water, his gaff hanging from his waistbelt, casting and recasting. He would wade out into the very middle of the Dee, trying to find the elusive salmon. But while he was there he was never successful. He did not have the luck to land a single fish. Yet there was no doubt that he was enjoying himself, forgetting for some time, at any rate, the responsibilities and cares of his high office. He must have had an immense stock of patience. He certainly needed it fishing there, for he would stand for many hours in some discomfort without having any reward for his trouble. This in spite of the salmon which occasionally leaped from the river almost within reach of his rod. I did actually see this happen. The look of disgust on the Prime Minister's face was remarkable to behold.

One occasion to which we always looked forward during our time at Balmoral was the famous Braemar Gathering held every year in the Princess Royal Park, part of the estate of the late Princess Royal, Duchess of Fife. Here is a wonderful setting for a Highland Gathering, flanked by hills and big mountains in the distance, with a flat plateau of vivid green grassland in the center. During August and September there are many other Highland Games' meetings held, at Aboyne, at Ballater, and elsewhere, but the Braemar Gathering is the definite Blue Riband event of the season. Every year without fail the Royal Family go to the Games. At the entrance to the games arena the Lord Lieutenant of the County, the Marquess of Aberdeen, meets the Royal visitors and escorts them to their pavilion, where various dignitaries are presented to them. Then they settle down to witness bagpipe contests, Highland dancing, including a sword dance, and Highland tests of strength and skill, like putting the weight, tossing the caber, throwing the hammer, wrestling and running contests, and displays by pipe bands.

King George V used to get a great deal of personal enjoyment from the games. King George VI regarded attendance at them, I think, rather as an official duty. But, with his keen sense of humor, he enjoyed some of the fun, especially when things went wrong, as they sometimes will even at the best regulated of games. I have seen him double up with laughter when a weight-putter has just thrown the weight the wrong way, and it has dropped a few inches from his own feet.

The Queen and Princess Margaret as little girls used to enjoy the Highland Games meeting very much indeed. They would attempt to escape from their nanny, the late Mrs. Knight, and run happily across the field, quite regardless of the danger of being struck by a hammer or a caber. Back at Balmoral Castle the two little girls would attempt to have a Highland Games meeting of their own, much to the alarm, sometimes, of their mother.

The Highland Games are usually held on the fourth or fifth of September toward the end of the Royal visit to Deeside. It can be very hot indeed at this time of year on Deeside, but it can also rain. When it does rain it is a torrential downpour. With low clouds obscuring the hills, and one of the famous Scotch mists creeping up to the games field, it can be very unpleasant.

I recall at least once hearing King George VI complain bitterly after returning from a visit to the Games in such bad weather conditions. Why, he wanted to know, could not the Royal visit to the Games be cut out of his program? When he recovered from his discomfort and displeasure, of course the King withdrew the suggestion. He knew very well that to withdraw Royal patronage from such an important gathering would be a bad thing. This is just another example of the way the Monarch's hands are tied and his or her actions are governed and bound by the rule of precedent.

But in fine weather the Games were a delightful afternoon's amusement. There was invariably plenty of refreshment for members of the Castle staff and for others attending the Games. It was always a matter of regret to King George and Queen Elizabeth, and certainly it is today to the Queen, when their visit to Deeside comes to an end and they have to leave the lovely Highlands.

It is true that members of the Royal Family have to work very hard indeed. I often hear people commenting on this and expressing sympathy for them. But if they do work hard, it is equally true that their work is set, and their lives are spent, among very pleasant surroundings, and there are a great many advantages in being a member of the Royal Family, particularly if you can spend some of your time at Balmoral or at Sandringham.

A very special Royal occasion stands out vividly in my memory. This was the birth of Prince Charles, the Heir to the Throne, at Buckingham Palace on the night of Sunday, November 14, 1948. Princess Elizabeth was in a room on the first floor, which had been converted into a sort of maternity ward. Her doctors were of course in constant attendance on her, and during Sunday afternoon we in Buckingham Palace knew that the birth was expected later that day. I have never seen King George VI and Queen Elizabeth so excited and nervous as they were that afternoon and late evening. The Duke of Edinburgh was nervous, too, but not more than they. The three of them did not seem to know what to do to pass the time, until at last the hour came when the doctors announced with great pleasure that the Princess had been safely delivered of an infant Prince. The King and Queen went at once to see their daughter and their new grandson. They were both delighted, and embraced their son-in-law in the corridor. Then Prince Philip, delighted beyond measure that his first child should be a son, gave orders that everyone in the Palace should have a glass of champagne to drink the new baby's health.

Strict precautions had been taken to keep the exact sequence of events at Buckingham Palace secret. This was because pressmen and Press photographers were maintaining a night-and-day vigil outside the Palace. The doctors, I remember, used to come into the Palace through the Electricians' Gate in Buckingham Palace Road, to avoid being noticed by the press-men. This Royal birth was historic, not only because it was the birth of a son in the direct line of succession to the throne, but because for the first time the birth of a future Heir to the Throne took place without the presence of the Home Secretary. Ever since a Court scandal in the days of Queen Anne, it had been the rule of the Home Secretary of the day to be present in the room where a Royal birth takes place, so that he can testify beyond doubt that the child is in fact the son or daughter of the Royal mother. In the days of King George V this custom had been slightly altered, so that the Home Secretary no longer went into the actual room where the birth was taking place, but stayed in an adjoining room, and was the first person to see the Royal infant after it had been delivered. The birth of Princess Margaret at Glamis Castle in 1930 was an exception to this rule. Mr. J. R. Clynes, the then Home Secretary, was staying at Airlie Castle nearby. By the time he had been summoned to Glamis and had arrived at the Castle, the new Princess was born.

King George VI reviewed this position several times during his reign and eventually decided that the days for such a meaningless piece of ceremonial, which was distasteful alike to the Royal Family and to the Home Secretary, had passed. So when the birth of Prince Charles was expected, the King consulted with his Cabinet advisers, and it was agreed that the old custom should be allowed to lapse.

Of course Princess Elizabeth herself was delighted beyond measure that her first-born was a son. Soon after she had recovered she gave orders that everyone in the Palace should be allowed to have a glimpse of the new baby. For the next day or two there was a constant procession of visitors to see Prince Charles sleeping peacefully in his cot in a room on the first floor. I thought he looked a delightful little boy as he lay there comfortably among his white covers, ignorant of the great future before him.

Now, for my last memory of Royal rejoicings, let me go forward to a certain day in June, 1953, when nearly all the world joined in the festivities that marked the Coronation of Her Majesty Queen Elizabeth II. To us in the Palace it was a day of intensely personal feelings, for we had helped with all the long preparations, and now our work had reached its climax....

"Isn't it wonderful?"

The Queen's eyes were aglow with excitement, a smile of sheer joy trembled all the time on her lips, and she seemed

to radiate happiness, as she walked slowly—oh, so slowly—
along the Grand Hall of Buckingham Palace, lined with the
men and women of her staff. Like her father, the Queen is
always thinking of others, especially of those who serve her,
be their jobs important or humble. She knew, no one better,
just how much hard work and long hours all of us had put
into the Coronation preparations in the past seven months.
She knew, too, how much we all envied the few privileged to
see her crowned in the Abbey. So she sent a message that
before she left in the State Procession for Westminster, she
would come to the Grand Hall and show herself to us before
anyone else in the outside world saw her in the glory of her
Coronation dress and jewelry.

I have never known a Royal message received with such
enthusiasm by the staff. It was a wonderful gesture from the
Queen. Everyone, even the old "Edwardians"—servants who
joined under Edward VII—and two "Old Vics"—men who
served under the great Queen, and who had been called out of
retirement to help—came to see the Queen. There was a gasp
of surprise, even from this audience, used to scenes of Royal
splendor, as the Queen appeared at the head of the Grand
Staircase and walked, with such easy, graceful dignity, down
its curving, red-carpeted steps. She looked the very personi-
fication of Royalty. I have seen members of the Royal
Family at close quarters in many different circumstances, in
moments of family joy or sorrow, at great occasions of State,
in formal robes and in country tweeds, but I have never seen
any one of them look so completely happy as the Queen did
then. Not even on her own wedding day, when we all called
her—with some justification—the Fairy Princess, did she
have quite the same air of supreme confidence to meet the
challenge of life.

"Isn't it wonderful?" she repeated, as she reached the end

of the line. She spoke in a half-whisper, almost like a child who sees her favorite fairy tale coming true. This was her last private moment before she faced the waiting millions outside, and she enjoyed it to the full. Below, in the body of the Grand Hall, the Great Officers of the Royal Household waited Her Majesty's pleasure. The tall Earl of Clarendon, the Lord Chamberlain, glanced once or twice at his watch, conscious of the exact timing of the procession, the minute-by-minute dovetailing of the whole day's program of pomp and ceremonial. King George VI, like his father, George V, never allowed himself to be a minute late "on parade." Would his daughter follow his example, or were we back to the days of Queen Alexandra, when half-hours mattered nothing?

I smiled to see the naval Press Secretary fussing round the Duke of Edinburgh, as he stood, handsome and debonair in his full-dress uniform of an Admiral of the Fleet. Apparently he did not entirely approve of some details of the Duke's dress. He adjusted the Duke's tunic, arranged his sword frog. But the Queen has an instinctive sense of time, almost as uncanny as her wonderful memory for faces and names, and she turned with a last smile for us just at the right moment to allow herself plenty of time to make her unhurried way to the great double glass doors, past the lovely Winterhalter portraits of her great-great-grandparents, Queen Victoria and Prince Albert, between the ranks of her curtsying Maids of Honor, past the bowing courtiers in their glittering gold-braided uniforms of State, past the line of her own Body-guards of Gentlemen-at-Arms and Yeomen of the Guard, to the waiting State Coach.

Long before she had entered it, many of us were rushing up the stone backstairs of the Palace to the roof, to command a view of the Mall, gay with its color, its triumphal archways, and its high suspended crowns, and to follow the Queen's progress through the biggest crowds I have seen, till the great gold coach, with its splendid train of Life Guards and Horse Guards and Court dignitaries, disappeared under Admiralty Arch, with the cheers of the crowds still borne to us on the faint breeze. It is a wonderful place from which to watch a Royal procession.

All the Queen's people cherish memories of that day of June 2, 1953, but to us in the Palace it was a special day of rejoicing. The Queen had given orders for everyone on the staff, from the highest of her State officials to the most humble of her servants, to be given champagne to drink her health. There was cold chicken for lunch in the Servants' Hall as well as in the Household Dining Room, but of course most of the chief officials—and as many of the staff as could possibly by hook or by crook obtain tickets—were at the Abbey. There, too, there was cold chicken, with salmon, lobster, cold meats, salads, fruit, and champagne for the Queen herself, her family, and her immediate circle of attendants and friends, to eat in the Abbey annex before the return drive to Buckingham Palace. The Queen is never a big eater, and drinks very little, save for an occasional glass of medium dry sherry before, or a glass of champagne with, her meal. With the nervous tension of her greatest experience just behind her, she scarcely touched any of the choice foodstuffs we had sent over from the Palace.

It was when she got home, after her wonderful drive through the cheering crowds, their enthusiasm little damped by the rain, that the Queen could at last relax. Even then her first thought was for others. When members of her suite bemoaned the bad weather, the Queen said, "I felt sorry for all those thousands of people, especially the children, getting soaked. I do hope they will be all right." Now the Grand Hall was filled with Royalties as the stream of guests coming from the Abbey to late lunch (it was ordered for 4 P.M., but the Queen and her two hundred guests did not sit down until four-thirty) began to arrive. Somehow, the story of Queen Salote and her irrepressible smile in the rain had preceded her, and there was a lot of good-humored banter between her and the other Royal personages. The Queen and her dusky fellow-monarch from Tonga seemed to have taken to each other at once, and it was charming to see the friendly looks of mutual admiration they exchanged.

As soon as she had made her appearance on the balcony with her family, the Queen's first act was to take off her crown. The Imperial Crown is much lighter than the Crown of St. Edward, used at the actual Coronation, but it is still a heavy burden to carry on your head for several hours. We were not surprised when Margaret MacDonald, the Queen's maid, told us the Queen complained of feeling rather tired, with a slight headache. Her mother, standing slightly in the background, watching with such obvious love and pride as her daughter moved regally among her guests, smiled with what must have been sympathetic memory. She had used almost those identical words after her own Coronation as Queen Consort sixteen years before.

CHAPTER NINE

The King in War

M<small>Y</small> <small>MOST</small> vivid memory of the King at war is on a day at Buckingham Palace in September, 1940. Bombs had fallen on the Palace in the morning. While the debris was still falling, and clouds of dust and smoke filled the air, I was below ground in the servants' corridor helping to clear away some of the mess. Suddenly I looked up to find a familiar slim figure clad in the blue-and-gold uniform of an Admiral of the Fleet at my side. It was the King. To my surprise, the back of his naval tunic and the bottom of his trousers and shoes were completely white. They were covered with brick dust where the King had been clambering through the ruins of the Royal private chapel demolished by bombs.

The revolting smell of cordite and bomb debris and gas from the burst mains combined to make the atmosphere extremely unpleasant.

The King and Queen ignored all this as they walked round several times talking to their servants and the Palace work-people, asking about their experiences and making sure that we were taking good care of them. Later that day the King and Queen went to a London district that had been heavily bombed the previous day. They walked round pitiful bombed homes talking to the homeless and the evacuated and the injured. None of the thousands of men and women who cheered their King and Queen as they visited them knew that their Royal visitors had themselves come from a bombed home.

The King and Queen took it all in their stride. It was a wonderful example to all of us at the Palace, and later when the facts became known, an encouragement to all the King's people. I believe it was two hundred years since a King of England had been under fire from his enemies.

The Royal Family are not given to superstition, but for the superstitious it may be interesting to record that the date of this raid was Friday the thirteenth of September. For the King and Queen, Friday the thirteenth was indeed a lucky day. Before they came down to investigate the damage they had been standing looking out of a big window on the first floor of the Palace above the King's Door, watching the German dive bomber approaching. On this occasion, as the King proudly boasted several times later to his friends, he and the Queen actually saw the bombs falling from the German plane. Little did they think that those bombs were directed at their Palace, until the missiles approached with tremendous rapidity. The King pulled the Queen away from the window and they crouched down on the red-carpeted corridor. Splintered glass from the window crashed around them and they might easily have been blinded by the glass. They escaped without a scratch of any kind.

Only later in the day did we hear of Their Majesties' escape. There was nothing whatever in their demeanor to show that they had so narrowly escaped injury or, perhaps, death. The German bomber approached the Palace from the direction of Wellington Barracks and St. James's Park. He dropped his bombs at such a point that they straddled the Palace, one of them scoring a direct hit on the private chapel, blowing the interior of it to a mass of rubble. Most of the servants below stairs had already taken refuge in their air-raid shelters, and

the kitchen staff were with them. Some of the officials of the
Royal Household were working at their desks on the ground
floor. One or two of these dived underneath their desks to
protect themselves. Not until many years later was the general public allowed to know of the narrow escape of the King
and Queen.

This was not the only time in which the King escaped
injury, and possible death, from a German bomb. One night,
when fortunately he was at Windsor, a bomb fell just in the
Palace quadrangle. Splinters of it penetrated some of the
rooms, including the downstairs apartment which the King
used as his bedroom when he slept in London. A large bomb
splinter several inches in length, with a jagged edge, went
through the room and pierced the wall wardrobe where the
King's uniforms were hung. Had the King been in the room,
it is almost certain that he would have been in the direct path
of the bomb splinter. When the Palace bomb damage was
repaired after the war, this particular wall was left, by the
King's personal orders, as it was. It was his own pet war
memento. So far as I know, that German bomb splinter is
still embedded in this wall of Buckingham Palace.

Like other Londoners, the King, after it had happened, was
"proud of his bombs." He would tell official visitors and guests
from overseas about the incident, describing vividly how it
had happened, and showing them the damage, the wrecked
Royal chapel, and other parts of the Palace. What most impressed the King was the fact that he and the Queen had
actually seen the bombs leaving the German plane before they
fell. "It was a direct attack on the Palace," the King used to
say. "There can be no doubt of that at all." His old home
across the road at 145 Piccadilly, just by Hyde Park Corner,
was wrecked in one of the early raids, when a German bomb
scored a direct hit on the house. The King was, in a way,

proud of this too. It made him one with all those of his people who had suffered from the bombs, and when he made his all-too-frequent tours of the badly bombed areas in London and the provinces, the King would often remark as he looked at wrecked homes, "You should see my house in Piccadilly. It just is not there any more!"

King George VI devoted all his energies and purpose in helping to win the war. He was above all things a very modest man, with no high ideas of his own abilities, tending always to under- rather than to overrate the importance of what he could do. But whatever Mr. Churchill or any of his other Ministers asked him to do, he did, at no matter how great the personal inconvenience, discomfort, or even danger. Mr. Herbert Morrison, the Minister of Home Security, was a favorite of the King's, and when he, with an instant perception of the effects on public morale both of the air raid and what he planned, telephoned the King on the night of the Coventry raid to suggest he should go up immediately to the stricken city, the King agreed at once. His Minister warned him there were almost certainly lots of unexploded bombs and land mines among the debris, so far not located, but the King waived all considerations of safety, and gave orders for his car (armor-plated with bullet-proof windows) to be ready at six the following morning.

When he came back that evening, the King's face was ashen and gray. He was horrified by what he had seen, and the memory of the still-smoking debris of the big city, and the ruins of the great cathedral, remained with him for the rest of his days. Those who were with him told me afterward how the King had walked through the ruins, talking to the A.R.P. squads and the homeless victims of the raid, ignoring the danger notices that lined his route. Several years later, it was found that the King's route had led him and his party over at least two unexploded land mines which might have blown up at any minute. When they told the King this, he smiled, and said it would be a good story for the history books. He told Queen Elizabeth about his adventures that evening, and the Queen's characteristic reaction was to say that she ought to have been there. As a result of this experience, it was arranged that on all future occasions the Queen should accompany the King, but Mr. Morrison suggested that Royal visits to the bombed areas should be delayed until the A.R.P. men had cleared a safe route. The King never fully approved of these precautions, but realized they were necessary, and took them with good grace.

While he knew his place was at home the King made no secret of his eagerness to go over to France with the invading troops once the attack on Europe had been launched. There were many important and obvious reasons why he should not go. He might be killed, wounded, or captured. But the King would listen to none of these, insisting that his troops had the right to expect him among them. Of all the King's departures from the Palace, this one he made on the evening of June 15, 1944, was the most secret. From the Palace the Royal car drove to Waterloo, where His Majesty boarded a special train which took him to Horsley in Surrey, where he spent the night on a quiet siding, experiencing, incidentally, a bad attack from the then almost-unknown flying bombs, many of which fell within an area of some miles from where the King was staying. This night journey was, of course, part of the elaborate security plan. It would have been perfectly easy for the King to go straight down in the morning to Portsmouth, where he was joining the cruiser *Arethusa* for the trip to Normandy, but the military security people thought this would be too obvious. That voyage across Channel was something the King was delighted to do. It compensated, in a way, for the feeling which we, who knew him well, realized sometimes came over him—a feeling of frustration at having to stay behind and watch others do the exciting things. He was trained as a naval officer, had his first experience under fire as a youth in 1916 in the Battle of Jutland, and it must sometimes have seemed hard to him that he could not take any active part in this war, particularly as he detested the Nazi regime and all it stood for.

The voyage across the Channel, even though mines and submarines made it one of some peril, and a day on the Normandy beaches well within range of the enemy guns were poor substitutes for an active part in the war, but it was at least something, and a measure of the King's personal feelings on this historic journey lies in what I heard afterward from those with him aboard *Arethusa* about his first "executive order" in the cruiser. It was a command to break the Royal Standard from the masthead—a simple enough order for the customary procedure when the Sovereign is aboard one of his ships, but it sent a shudder through the security-minded Royal entourage. After all the secrecy precautions, here was the King advertising his presence aboard the ship, plain for the enemy to see. One or two senior officers tried to argue with the King, but to no avail. The standard was hoisted as the cruiser passed through a flotilla of mine sweepers lying anchored just outside Portsmouth Harbor, and remained flying throughout the trip to the beach-heads, and on the return journey that evening. It was a personal gesture of defiance from King George VI to his enemies, and every man aboard *Arethusa* felt a surge of pride at the action. So did the men of the mine sweepers, whose cheers when they found the King was among them at their war stations were some of the loudest, I was told, he heard in the whole war.

One of the most interesting features of Palace life during

the war were the weekly luncheons which the King gave to his great Prime Minister, Mr. (now Sir Winston) Churchill. Every Tuesday the King set aside two hours for conference with his Prime Minister. But instead of being an ordinary audience where the King would see the Premier in his business room, special arrangements were made. Ever thoughtful of others, the King, realizing that Mr. Churchill's time was the most valuable of anyone's in the whole of the Commonwealth, arranged things so that the Prime Minister could give him the maximum of information with the minimum of dislocation of his own timetable.

This problem was solved by the King by arranging that every Tuesday the Prime Minister should lunch with him. It was obviously essential that they should lunch alone, and the King gave orders for us to provide a self-service lunch. It was always at about a quarter to one that the Prime Minister drove up to Buckingham Palace in his car. As he got out, nearly always smoking a long cigar, he would turn and give his familiar V-sign to any of the crowds outside the Palace gates. Then he would enter the Palace and walk along the red-carpeted corridor to the King's apartments on the ground floor.

The King did not care for cold lunches, so the Chef provided simple dishes like grilled fish or a grilled leg of chicken for him and his guest. The King and Mr. Churchill helped themselves. On a sideboard in the small sitting room adjoining what is known at the Palace as the Caernarvon Room, where these meeting were held, were assorted cold meats, cigarettes, small decanters containing whisky for the King, and brandy for the Prime Minister, and always two or three of the finest cigars from the Palace stock for Mr. Churchill. These meetings rarely lasted less than two hours, sometimes longer.

While the King and his Prime Minister were closeted together in the Caernarvon Room, the Page of the Presence on duty would take up his position outside the big double doors, to guard against any chance intrusion. Not even the Queen was allowed to be present at these most secret of talks. On Tuesdays she and any members of the Royal Family who happened to be at the Palace lunched separately in another room. Those Tuesday luncheons, by the way, allowed those of us in the Palace to get a hint of several vital war secrets. If, when Tuesday came round, orders were for Royal lunch to be served as usual, we knew that the Premier was not coming to see the King. That meant one of two things: either Mr. Churchill was ill, or he was off on some vital mission taking him out of the country. Nothing else was important enough to cause the Tuesday Palace visit to be canceled.

I always made a point of being up in the well of the Grand Entrance on Tuesday afternoon to see the Prime Minister take his departure. He would walk down the three carpeted steps of the Grand Hall to his waiting car, nearly always looking rather serious, but vigorous and full of confidence. To me, and any of my colleagues who watched him, these glimpses of our war leader were most inspiring. I am sure that they had much the same effect on the King. However grave the situation—and no one in the whole of the Commonwealth worried more about the course of the war, nor did anyone know more about the real truth behind the communiqués—the King always looked cheerful and confident after a meeting with his Prime Minister.

I have been told, indeed, that this weekly meeting with the Prime Minister helped tremendously to keep the King going throughout the war years. To some extent the help was mutual. Mr. Churchill was immensely heartened by his Sovereign's confidence in him, and there was a great friendship and mutual admiration between the two men. At the end of the war the King offered Sir Winston Churchill the highest honor in his power to bestow: the Knighthood of the Garter. Sir Winston, for reasons of his own, asked the King's permission to be allowed to decline the honor, and he continued to be known as Mr. Winston Churchill until the end of the King's reign.

Many people have wondered why the Prime Minister reversed his decision at the beginning of the reign of Queen Elizabeth II. We always understood at Buckingham Palace that the Queen, when she was Princess Elizabeth, conceived an enormous admiration for her father's great Prime Minister, and once said to him, "If you are Prime Minister when I become Queen, I would like you to be my first Garter Knight." Mr. Churchill told the young Princess that it would give him great delight to accept such an honor from her if that day ever came. So it was that the first Garter Knight to be created by Queen Elizabeth II was the man who had been her father's Prime Minister and who had declined the same honor from him.

Buckingham Palace in 1940, that first year of the real war after the end of the "phony" war, became a sort of refuge camp for all the exiled Royalty of Europe. The first to arrive, I remember, were King Haakon of Norway and his son, Crown Prince Olaf, with their secretaries and aides-de-camp. King George VI went to Liverpool Street Station to welcome his Royal uncle in exile. All this, of course, was done in the closest of wartime secrecy. Like other war refugees, the Norwegian King and his son and their suite arrived in London with just the clothes that they were wearing and nothing else. The first thing that King George VI did was to tell his valet to sort out whatever clothes they wanted from his own wardrobe. Shirts, socks, ties, etc., were all loaned to King Haakon and Crown Prince Olaf until later they could be fitted out by the King's tailor with uniforms and clothes. The King detached a valet from his own staff to be in personal attendance on his uncle and his cousin. The first thing that King Haakon and his son wanted when they reached the Palace, I recall, was a hot bath. Then they were conducted to rooms on the ground floor which the King put at their disposal for as long as they wanted to stay at the Palace.

Later on, King Haakon found headquarters for himself in London, but he continued to call at Buckingham Palace every week. The reason for this weekly visit was a singularly un-Royal one. King Haakon used to come and collect his own laundry. There was a peculiar reason behind this. It was that the actual whereabouts of King Haakon were a very closely guarded secret indeed. It was thought best that the laundry which did his washing should not know where their Royal customer was living. Of course he could have sent a messenger to pick up his laundry, but for some reason of his own the tall, friendly Norwegian King preferred to call at the Palace and collect it. Many were the laughs and jokes that he had with the servants at the Privy Purse Door as he walked in to pick up the laundry box. Of all the Royal personages I have met before, during, and after the war I have never known any so democratic and friendly in his approach and so easy to get on with as King Haakon.

The next Royal refugee to come seeking sanctuary at Buckingham Palace was Queen Wilhelmina of the Netherlands. She had had a really terrible time. After being chased across her country by the advancing German hordes, she crossed the North Sea in a destroyer, only to be bombed on the way by German Stukas and other aircraft. She, too, arrived at Buckingham Palace with literally nothing except the clothes she was wearing.

I remember vividly walking through the Grand Hall the first morning after her arrival. As I was going to an equerry's office in order to deal with some minor point, I saw coming toward me an elderly lady, small of stature but very stout. She was walking extremely slowly, and looking tired-out. As I drew closer I thought it must be some housemaid whom I did not recognize. It was not until she bowed to me in a foreign manner, and said good morning in broken English, that I realized who it must be. I quickly returned her bow, and, standing on one side, watched her go slowly through the Caernarvon Room and the open French windows out onto the terrace. It was a lovely summer's morning, and she sat there in the sunshine just, it seemed to me, drinking in the peaceful atmosphere. Many a morning afterward I saw her sitting in the same deck chair, which had been specially provided for her in that spot. But never did I see her either pick up a book to read, or a piece of paper to write on. She just sat quite still, with her hands folded on her lap, gazing across the lawn toward the lake. It seemed to me to be a most pathetic sight to watch a reigning queen sitting there with apparently no interest at all in life, content just to be alive. I think Queen Wilhelmina was quite stunned after her terrifying experiences and the frightening journey to England. It was not until many days had passed that the Dutch Queen recovered some of her normal serenity and began to take up the threads of life again.

These foreign Royal refugees had to have ration books, and I remember going to the Westminster Food Office to arrange for the ration books for King Haakon, Crown Prince Olaf, and Queen Wilhelmina. Each time I had to take the books up to their suite for signature. It was just my luck when I took King Haakon's to him to encounter one of his aides-de-camp who could not speak a word of English, and, of course,

I had no Norwegian. But we both managed to make ourselves understood, pointing and gesticulating with our hands. I think that this must be the only occasion in history on which a Royal signature has been obtained purely by the use of sign language. But I soon got the requisite signature, took the documents back to the Westminster Food Office, and all was well.

Buckingham Palace throughout the war was just as strictly rationed as any other house in the country. At the very beginning of hostilities the King issued his command that we should all fall into line with everyone else and receive no favors. Everyone, from the King and Queen downward, had his own ration books. These books, Royal and otherwise, were kept in a safe in my own office, and it was part of my duty to remove the appropriate coupons from them each week and send these on to the Food Office. This was the same practice as was adopted in the big hotels for their guests. When the King and Queen wanted to give a special party, or entertain any very important guests, it was another part of my job to go across to the Westminster Food Office and negotiate for the necessary extra rations. But here again, by the King's personal orders, no special favors were asked for. Margarine, not butter, was mostly served at Buckingham Palace in those days, except at the Royal table itself, where butter from the farms at Windsor was consumed in small quantities.

From the first day of the war until the last the King wore uniform every day except when he was in the country, at Windsor, or at Sandringham, when he would change into gray flannels and a sports jacket. He wore naval, military, and R.A.F. uniform in turn, choosing each for the occasion to which it was appropriate. But his favorite was the undress uniform of an Admiral of the Fleet, and indeed this was the uniform that became him most. The Queen decided at the beginning of the war not to wear uniform. Many people urged on her the desirability of wearing it, since she was the head of the three women's services, in name if not in fact. But the Queen was adamant on the point.

All of us at Buckingham Palace had to come under the National Registration Act. It was the King's wish that all men working at the Palace should join up, if they had to, in the proper groups. The King's chauffeur, for example, was enrolled in the Royal Horse Guards. He did his training, and eventually was promoted to be a Corporal of Horse. For the rest of the war he drove the King in his khaki uniform with his three chevrons of rank on his sleeve. It may seem that this was just an idle gesture, but there was a definite purpose behind the King's orders. Frequently the King had to go into some most secret army headquarters and other places where no civilians were allowed. And the fact that his chauffeur was a member of the armed forces made it easy for him to drive the King wherever he had to go. The King's valet, Tom Jerram, joined up. He was enrolled in the Grenadier Guards, and went through the Guards training at Caterham Depot, coming back to Buckingham Palace delighted to be serving his Royal master once more. For the rest of the war he wore khaki. And there was not a better-pressed battledress in the whole of the Brigade of Guards than that worn by Mr. Jerram!

I, too, came under joining-up orders and I was told that the King wanted me to join the Royal Berkshire Regiment. I therefore went one morning to a recruiting office to take my medical examination. At the recruiting office I went through this ritual, and filled in the necessary attestation forms. Then I was taken before a major who knew that I was from Buckingham Palace. He asked me many questions in connection with my duties there. After he had gone into this in a great deal of detail, he looked me up and down and said, "Ah, lorry-driving for you." I nearly burst out laughing. After all, if I was to go join the Army, I could be very useful indeed in the Catering Corps, since my job suited me entirely for that branch of the service, whereas I had never driven a lorry in my life, so it seemed to me that it was going to be a great waste of time teaching Corbitt to become a driver. However, it was not my place to ask, and in any case I knew just what was going to happen to me, by the King's orders. Later that same day I was transferred to Class W.2 Reserve, and was able to return to Buckingham Palace still in my lounge suit, though I was now a fully fledged private in the famous Royal Berkshire Regiment!

Another amusing incident in connection with the call-up occurred to the Royal Chef, Mr. Ronnie Aubrey. When he came back to the Palace after making his attestation for the Royal Air Force, he was furious. At least they treated him with some degree of intelligence, for he was transferred to the catering department. But he was stationed at Cardington, and there the job they found for the man who cooked for the King in civil life was to make cocoa for the various messrooms. Aubrey, a mild-tempered man who can always see the funny side of things, laughed afterward, but at the time he was very indignant. But his period of service with his unit was short and he soon returned to Buckingham Palace. Others of the King's mess did normal service for the rest of the war and the Palace was run on a very small staff.

Soon after the beginning of the war I was summoned with some secrecy into the presence of a very high official of the Court, who told me that he had personal orders for me from the King. It was a special security job. I was told for the first time of the existence of Establishment "A," which I discovered to be a large mansion in the West country which was to be prepared as a refuge for the Royal Family in case heavy bombing or other enemy action made it necessary for them to leave London. My duty was to go down to this house and make preliminary arrangements. Early in 1940 I went there without telling even my wife where I was going. For two days and nights I stayed at the house, scouting round the village and the nearby countryside to investigate shopping facilities. No one except the owner of the house himself knew where I came from, and therefore I had to disguise my real intentions. I had great fun walking into a butcher's in the village and then into a poulterer's and telling the manager or owner that I had some very special business. Privately I said to them, "In the event of some V.I.P.'s coming down here at some distant date without much advance notice, would it be possible for you to supply me with certain foods?" Then I would explain that the total number would be perhaps thirty-five or forty, and that I should want all sorts of cuts of meat, loins and shoulders of lamb, a weekly sirloin of beef with the fillet attached—this was the King's particular choice. The look of astonishment on the shopkeepers' faces was something to remember. I found a fishmonger, too, and asked if he would be able to supply me with whiting, halibut, turbot, Dover sole, salmon, lobster, and crab—an order which staggered him.

Already a great load of emergency stores had been sent down by rail from Buckingham Palace and Windsor Castle. The bulk stores in heavy cases which traveled on the railway direct from a London grocery firm were addressed to me personally at the house. Some of the other goods which came from the Palace or from Windsor Castle were simply marked, Establishment "A." All these precautions were necessary to preserve the complete secrecy of the Royal plan. It was therefore with a great deal of annoyance as well as amusement that while I was at the house I discovered a piece of carelessness which could easily have given the whole show away to any enemy agent who happened to be around. There was a large quantity of bedding, mattresses, and some furniture, which was sent from Windsor Castle for use in the staff quarters at Establishment "A." It was very late in the day when the lorry containing them turned up. Eventually it came to a halt in the yard of the house. I went with the driver round to the back of the lorry and he undid the tailboard. The owner of the big house, a man of title, and his lady were with us. They were just as horrified as I was to discover that every article in the lorry was roped up in canvas packing and bore a large yellow label with a black crown, and the words in black letters, "ROYAL MEWS." Someone at Windsor had blundered.

The Royal Housekeeper from Buckingham Palace, Mrs. Ferguson, joined me to make final arrangements for the comfort of the staff and the suite, as well as for the Queen and the Princesses, if they came down. We did not, of course, know then exactly what the Royal plans were, but when I motored back to Buckingham Palace I wrote a lengthy report of every detail of my mission, including the full story of the labeled packages. All was now in readiness in case the Royal Family had to be evacuated. Those members of the Palace staff who were to travel with the Royal Family had each been told, under the most solemn oaths of secrecy, the part they were to play in the plan. After my experience with the local shopkeepers I have often wondered what would have happened had the plan been put into operation and members of the Royal Family with their staffs descended on the quiet little village hidden in the West country.

All this took place early in 1940, and it seemed to many of us, including myself, to be just another rather silly precaution, because we were still in the period of the "phony war."

But after Dunkirk the possibility of the Royal Family evacuating to the West country became a very likely event. Once more I was called in to a high official's office, and again with pledges of the utmost secrecy, I was told that it would be my job to travel down to Establishment "A" with the Queen and the two Princesses and remain there with them in charge of the Household Supply Department and to deal with the situation in the best way that I could for as long as it was necessary. This plan, I was told, would be put into effect in the event of further heavy bombing on London, or if there were any invasion. At no time, so far as I know, did the King plan to leave London himself. It was his intention to stay in the capital, or wherever his Government went, while his wife and children were evacuated to comparative safety. But fortunately the changing tide of war rendered it unnecessary to put the plan into operation.

Four years later, in 1944, when it was apparent that we were going to win the war, and the dangers alike of invasion and of V-1 and V-2 bombs had passed, I was again sent down to that country house in the West country, this time with a much happier mission. It was my job to arrange for the return of the stores which had been transferred there four years before. I made out a list of every item for return to the Palace stores and had every other case opened to test the contents. It was a remarkable tribute, I thought, to the makers of tinned goods that almost everything had kept extremely well. One or two tins of ham had "blown," but all the other tinned goods were in excellent condition: the sardines, the pilchards, the bacon, the brisket of beef, the luncheon meat, and so on.

Everything that was in fat or oil was in excellent condition, but the large jars of turtle soup and turtle meat which had been included for use at the Royal table had gone bad. I opened several of the tins and each smelled awful. There was nothing to do but throw them away. All the tinned fruit and jams—of which there were many, many pounds—were in first-class condition. There were tinned tongues too, and these were excellent, but the twenty-eight bags of lump sugar had softened into a sticky mess. These I handed over to the lady of the house for jam-making.

It was during the Balmoral trip in 1938 that we had our first foretaste of things to come. Civil Defence Officers came to the Castle and stayed with us for two or three days, taking the measurements of everyone in residence for the fitting of gas masks. The King and Queen and everyone in the Castle, down to the last-joined member of the staff, were measured and fitted. Specially made gas masks were provided for the Princesses. Princess Margaret, then a tiny tot of eight, was delighted with hers, I remember. She seemed to regard it as a sort of new plaything, not realizing the horrid significance of it. A year later, when we were at Balmoral again, the King suddenly left for London. A few days later he was followed by the Queen. War had been declared.

The rest of the Castle inhabitants, including Princess Elizabeth and Princess Margaret, stayed there. A few days later instructions came from the King at Buckingham Palace that we were all to pack up and go to London. The last job we had to do was to make arrangements for the two Princesses to stay at Birkhall, the small dower house near Balmoral, which the King and Queen had used as their Scottish home in their days as Duke and Duchess of York. Special beds and mattresses were sent across from Balmoral to Birkhall for the Princesses' use. A small number of the Royal staff were left behind to look after the Princesses, with the King's naval equerry, an old personal friend—Captain, later Sir, Harold Campbell, a hero of the Zeebrugge raid of World War I—in charge. A Sergeant of the Metropolitan Police, with a few constables, a chauffeur with a car, and a shooting brake were also left at Birkhall for the use of the Princesses and their governess, Miss Marion Crawford.

At that time no one knew what course the war would take. It was the King's intention to leave his daughters in the comparative security and safety of the Highlands for as long as seemed necessary. As it happened, the Princesses stayed at Balmoral on their own for a very short time. Before Christmas that year the King decided that it was safe to bring them south, and they traveled to Sandringham to join their father and mother for their first wartime Christmas. But it was Princess Elizabeth's great delight to be the "head of the household" at Balmoral, as the person of the highest rank staying there. She retains to this day a proof of that experience, because her identity card, issued in Scotland, bears the figure "1" in the final column.

Leaving the Princesses behind in the autumn glories of Balmoral, the officials of the Royal Household and the rest of the staff left at 5 p.m., on the evening of Saturday, September 2, and traveled to Windsor by a special train, the windows of which had already been blacked out. It was my first experience of wartime travel, and it seemed a very long and tiring journey south, as we were shunted from one line to another during the night. We did not know that war had been declared until we stopped at Wolverhampton on Sunday morning and heard the news. As we traveled onward through the day I could see the barrage balloons already up.

When we reached Windsor that evening, I found that it had been decided that the Castle should be made the Royal headquarters for the duration. Buckringham Palace came under the evacuation scheme. Everything had been sent down by Army lorry in advance from the Palace. The private secretary's offices, the accounts offices, the treasurer's departments, all the other working rooms of the Palace had been emptied. At Windsor Castle there were masses of boxes, files, ledgers, typewriters, and other office equipment, all waiting to be put into their new quarters. There was confusion among the Royal staff as we sorted out the various rooms and put temporary labels on their doors. I went back to Buckingham Palace on the following Monday to have a look round, and it was a sad sight that met my eyes. All the chandeliers in the State Rooms had been taken down and carefully packed in protective material, and taken away for safe storage.

All the art treasures of the Palace had been taken away, packed, numbered and catalogued, and buried in caves in the country for the duration. Extra precautions were taken to protect these priceless paintings and I am very glad to say that when they were brought back to Buckingham Palace and unpacked at the end of the war, not one of them had suffered any damage. With the aid of a master-plan, they were rehung in exactly the positions they had occupied before the war.

In those early days I was deeply moved to see all the lovely furniture of the State Rooms packed away, the drawing rooms emptied of their beautiful pieces of chinaware and other objects of art. It was all desolate and depressing. Below stairs, I found the strong room, known as the Gold Plate Room, where the Yeoman of the Silver Pantry looks after the State collection of gold tableware and ornaments, empty. The senior and very trusted servant who looks after the gold plate has to become almost an expert goldsmith himself once he is given this job, for he must, with his assistants, take apart, clean, and reassemble all the intricate pieces of gold plate whenever there is a State banquet or other occasion for their use. No one at Buckingham Palace, as far as I have ever been able to discover, knows why the servant in charge of the gold plate should be known as the Yeoman of the Silver Pantry, but so it is.

The gold plate had been packed into large cases and sent out of London. As with the pictures, when the gold plate was brought back to Buckingham Palace and unpacked after the war, it was found to have suffered no damage. It had been specially wrapped in wax paper and other protective material, including felt. The plate was brought back to Buckingham Palace one day in 1946 on Army lorries with a special police escort on motorcycles. Every piece, as we expected, was very badly discolored. It took the Yeoman of the Silver Pantry and his assistants many months of hard work cleaning, polishing with jewelers' rouge, and submitting the plate to baking processes before it was properly restored. I remember thinking, when I first saw it gleaming under the rose light of the great chandeliers in the State Ballroom at the first big banquet which the King and Queen gave at the end of the war, "This is really peace and victory." Buckingham Palace then seemed to me to have become its old self again, and I realized, as I had done at no other moment, that the war was indeed over and things were back, if not to normal, at least to something approaching normality.

At Windsor Castle, A.R.P. Control Rooms were set up in the basement some time before war was declared, and a Home Guard Unit was being formed. There was also a Home Guard Unit at Buckingham Palace, with Mr. Williams, the Superintendent of the Palace, in command. This was known as the Buckingham Palace Company of the Westminster Home Guard. At Windsor, too, a workshop was set up in the Castle basement at the King's command. Here precision parts for guns were made, and the King himself, as well as many members of his Household and many of the staff, took a hand in the evenings at turning the lathes and manufacturing these important pieces of armament.

For the first two months of the war there was much work going on at Windsor Castle fitting out special air-raid shelters for the Royal Family. Blacking out the hundreds of windows at the Castle was itself a major task, and took many weeks to complete. There was no question of hoarding at Windsor Castle or at Buckingham Palace, but reasonable precautions had to be taken, and for many months stores had been accumulated at both places. Everything had been done to ensure that for some weeks, at any rate, the Castle and the Palace could be self-sufficient in supplies if enemy action were to cut them off from the rest of the country.

In those early days the King made daily journeys to London, usually wearing a Field Marshal's uniform. He would go to Buckingham Palace to receive members of his War Cabinet in audience, to discuss affairs with his Generals, Admirals, and Air Marshals, and to visit various Ministries. Life went on pleasantly enough at Windsor Castle, and there was little in the air to remind us that we were, in fact, at war. Late in December, at only a few days' notice, we were told that the King had decided to spend Christmas at Sandringham. I began my usual routine, making the arrangements for removal of the Court, but it did not seem the same this time. In the peaceful grounds of Sandringham, associated always in my mind with Royal Christmas holidays, soldiers in khaki were on duty guarding the various gates; there were barbed-wire entanglements, with tin cans dangling from them, across the paths and drives; light antiaircraft guns were in position on the private Royal golf course; and the house itself had been blacked out.

Thorough in everything he did, the King was determined that his homes should be examples to the rest of his subjects, and we all received explicit instructions that the King himself would be most angry if any member of his staff was ever found to have infringed the black-out regulations.

It was during this stay at Sandringham that I had my first experience of food rationing. From Sandringham House I drove over in one of the Household cars to a little village called Docking, a few miles away. Here I met the local food officers. To these officers I had to give the full numbers of the Royal Family, their guests, the Household officials and staff. I also had to arrange with them that Sandringham House should be registered as a catering establishment, so that we might have the same facilities as a hotel, a restaurant, or a factory, to obtain necessary permits when the King wanted to entertain guests or when official visitors came to his residence bringing with them their suites, secretaries, and servants. All this was arranged without any difficulty. Indeed, I would like to pay tribute here to the work of the food officers in Norfolk, at Westminster, at Aberdeen, at Windsor, and wherever we went. They were always most helpful. I think that part of this was due not only to their loyalty to the King, but also to their appreciation of the fact that we from Buckingham Palace, acting on the King's own orders, never asked for anything more than our fair share, or for anything but what we were entitled to have.

The Household staff was now depleted of many of its younger members who had been called up. The remaining members of the staff, nearly all of whom held rank in one or the other of the three Services, donned uniform. They were indeed on Active Service, seeing that they were at the King's side, and it was for this reason that they were entitled to, and indeed ordered to, wear uniform throughout the war. All the while at Sandringham the King was transacting his daily State duties as usual. When the time came, in the middle of

January, for the Court to leave Sandringham, the King decided that he would have a portion of Buckingham Palace opened again. Up to now from the beginning of the war the Palace had been closed. Some of the Royal staff, including myself and many of the people immediately under me, were told to return to London to get the Palace ready for the Royal Family's return. At the Palace we organized our own roof-spotting system, our fire watchers, stretcher bearers, and staff sleeping shelters. There was a special system of bells to give air-raid warnings, and all of us, including the King himself and the Queen, were rehearsed in the drill of proceeding down to the special air-raid shelters allotted to each.

The King now took to coming up to the Palace early in the morning and staying till late in the evening. He traveled in a special armored car, driven by a military officer. But always with the King was one civilian—his faithful police officer, Chief Superintendent Hugh Cameron, now retired. For security reasons, the King returned to Windsor Castle to sleep every night. I understand that although he himself would not have minded staying in the capital, his Cabinet advised him to go back to Windsor each night because of the greater safety afforded him there. When the King did have to remain in London late in the evening, as happened many times, he ordered that his dinner should be served in the special air-conditioned shelter which had been built for him deep below ground. In this shelter, probably the safest in England apart from the shelters below ground at the Citadel over in White-hall, where the Cabinet could meet and work in safety, there were telephones with lines direct to the War Office and No. 10 Downing Street and to Windsor Castle as well. The King always set a good example to everyone by using this shelter, and he frequently made inquiries to see if the members of his staff were doing likewise.

Later in the war, when the flying bombs were exploding over London, the King held at least one Investiture in this same shelter. It was the strangest Investiture of any in history, with Knights kneeling before their King, if not on the field of battle, at least in a shelter from the enemy's weapons overhead, for the Investiture took place during an alert, with flying bombs passing in the immediate vicinity.

As the country settled down to life under wartime conditions the King and Queen gradually evolved a plan of life to meet the new circumstances. At Buckingham Palace one new feature was introduced into the Royal life in the form of little afternoon tea parties which the King and Queen gave to Red Cross organizations, to Service Chiefs, and to Cabinet Ministers. These parties took place on the ground floor in the Grand Hall, in order to make it easy to get down to the air-raid shelters should there be a sudden warning, as happened on more than one occasion. Two long buffet tables, each forty feet in length, were set up in the Grand Hall, left and right of the staircase leading to the Grand Entrance. Extra tea, sugar, and margarine, but no butter, were obtained under permits from the Westminster Food Office; and sandwiches, made with paste, prepared by the King's Chef from grouse shot at Balmoral, tomatoes, cucumbers and cress and other un-rationed commodities, were provided for the Royal guests.

Two hundred and fifty to three hundred people would be invited to the bigger of these parties. The Grand Hall would be thronged with men and women in uniform. The King and Queen would walk about in the middle of them separately, the King usually going down one side of the hall while the Queen went down the other. The parties would last for two and a half hours, from four until about 6:30 P.M., and they were a most successful innovation. Many hundreds, if not thousands, of people who had never met the King and Queen before had an opportunity of talking to them at these very informal functions. I have seen many famous people at these parties. I remember young King Peter of Yugoslavia, a slim, not very impressive figure in his uniform; the much more impressive and robust figure of General Dwight Eisenhower, in the American khaki; Mr. Winston Churchill, appearing more than once in the blue uniform of the Royal Air Force; Marshal of the Royal Air Force Lord Portal; Marshal of the Royal Air Force Lord Tedder; Field Marshal Lord Alexander; Field Marshal Lord Montgomery; General de Gaulle; and a score of others.

One party I remember was of a somewhat different kind. This was for some selected officers and men from the American Forces. The Queen always took a personal interest in the organization of these parties and would frequently send suggestions to me for the menu. For this American occasion she ordered that coffee should be served American style, instead of tea. She also gave orders that the Americans should be supplied with their own brand of toasted tobacco cigarettes, which I obtained through the kindness of the United States Embassy.

This party was a huge success. A number of American nurses were present and the Queen afterward expressed her admiration for the intelligence and charm of these women.

These informal parties, for there was nothing of a State occasion about them, were an entirely new feature of Buckingham Palace life. They were inspired by the Queen, whose easy charm of manner assures the success of any social gathering at which she is present.

King George VI, with his innate shyness, at first did not seem to enjoy this type of party, but after one or two had been held he took to the idea and enjoyed them as much as anyone, laughing and talking with his guests in a completely spontaneous manner. It was a pleasure indeed to see him so happy.

Royal servants, in their battledress livery, stood behind the long trestle tables handing out cups of coffee or tea and sandwiches and cakes. Officials of the Court were present too, officially in attendance on the King and Queen, but actually the King and Queen walked around with complete informality.

At the end of the war Princess Elizabeth in the khaki of an A.T.S. officer and, on one or two occasions, Princess Margaret, also came to these parties. It was their introduction to what we used to call the "semi-official" side of Court life, functions which were neither private family parties nor official State occasions. Both the Princesses, of course, enjoyed these parties, particularly Princess Margaret, to whom it gave her first opportunity of mixing freely with other people.

The American party itself was also an idea of the Queen's. Ever since the Royal visit to Canada and the United States before the war Queen Elizabeth has had a great liking for Americans and Canadians and never attempted to make any secret of her belief that the future of the world is inextricably bound up in the friendship betwen the great American and British people. So when the Americans came to England in the war to fight at our side, it was the Queen's delight to arrange as many meetings with them as she could. At American Air Force bases in many parts of the country she had met officers and men on visits with the King. Now she thought it would be a great gesture if the King invited some of his American allies to his own home in London.

To judge by the excited questions and the enormous interest of the American visitors in every single aspect of the Palace life, the Royal party left a very deep impression on them. I imagine that there must be tales still told in the states of the Far West as well as on the Atlantic Coast of "the day I had tea with the King and Queen of England." It was a gesture of international friendship which has borne very good fruit in subsequent days.

This lessening of formality in Palace parties was just one aspect of the gradual change in Palace life brought about almost imperceptibly by King George VI and his Queen to keep Royal ways abreast of the change in the life outside Buckingham Palace. A party of this kind would have been unthinkable in the days of King George V. The division and barrier between the Monarch and his people was much more strictly defined in those days. It was the genius of King George VI, aided and inspired by Queen Elizabeth, that he was able, not to remove this indispensable barrier, but to lower it so that there could be a new relationship of friendliness and affection established between the Sovereign and the people. It is on this foundation, I am sure, that the British Monarchy exists in its strength today.

All sorts of jobs came my way, but we were all anxious to keep the Palace running as well as we could and to do everything in our power to help the King and Queen. It was teamwork all the time, and no one complained.

What seemed at first to be a very easy task was given me at Christmas, 1942. The King was going to give his cousin, Lord Louis Mountbatten, a special present. It was an adjustable desk lamp which had been ordered direct from the manufacturers at Redditch. I was given the job of arranging for its collection from Paddington Station and delivering it to Lord Louis Mountbatten at his London flat during one of his few brief periods of leave from the Navy. Nothing, I thought, could be easier. On Christmas Eve I had heard nothing from the manufacturers, so I telephoned them from Buckingham

Palace to ask what had happened to the parcel. They told me that the lamp had been packed specially and addressed personally to me, and placed on a certain train. They told me the time the train was due to arrive in London. As I put the receiver down, the telephone rang again. It was an inquiry from the King at Windsor Castle, who wanted to know if his Christmas parcel had yet been delivered. As soon as I had finished talking to the Castle I left the Palace in a taxi to go to Paddington Station. I called on the station master and explained my business. He was most helpful, and told me if I went to the Parcels Department I would be able to pick up my parcel.

When I got to the Parcels Office I was astounded. There was a mountainous pile of boxes and packages over which a number of women porters were climbing trying to sort them out. It seemed pretty hopeless to expect them to find that single parcel addressed to me. I summoned up my courage and in my most diplomatic manner asked one of the women porters if she had happened to see a box, rather longer than it was broad, with my name on it. The girl paused and looked at me. For a moment there was silence, then in a torrent of pure Cockney she let forth, telling me exactly what she thought of people who came at such a time asking for one single parcel when there were "thausands" of packages that had been there for two or three days and were still waiting to be sorted out.

"Let me have a look for myself," I said, without much hope. I stepped forward and, believe it or not, the first parcel I put my hands on was the one I wanted. The woman porter looked with amazement. "Strewth!" she exclaimed, "I reckon you must be a magician, as well as coming from the Palace."

From the station I took the parcel to the flat where Lord

Mountbatten was staying and delivered it. Then I went back to Buckingham Palace and put through a call to Windsor Castle. I left a message to be given immediately to the King that the lamp hunt had ended happily and that his Christmas present had been delivered.

CHAPTER TEN

Four Reigns

As I came down from my bedroom in the Bachelors' Wing at Sandringham House on that February morning in 1952, I stopped suddenly, a chill of fear in my spine. I saw an early-morning calling tray. On it, beside the small silver teapot, stood a solitary cup of fine white china bearing the Royal cipher and crown in gold, and a plate bearing two thin slices of brown bread and butter with which the King invariably started the day. But the tray stood untouched on the floor outside the door of the King's bedroom. The time was after half-past eight so I knew there was something very wrong. Not once since he came to Buckingham Palace fifteen years before had I known King George VI fail to take his tea and bread and butter within a few minutes of its being taken in to him at 7:30 A.M., except when he was ill. A few moments later I met Jimmy MacDonald, the King's second valet, white-faced and trembling. He told me what I had already guessed—our Royal master was dead.

King George's death, though we had known for two years that it was coming, was a deep personal grief. The night before I had seen him at dinner talking and laughing in the best of spirits with the Queen and half a dozen house guests. Ever since his leg operation in the spring of 1949, the King had been but a shadow of his old self. He tired easily, and it was no surprise that night when, after a day of rough shooting in the woods, he slipped quietly off to bed immediately after dinner, leaving the Queen to take the party down to the ballroom for a film show.

At seven-thirty in the morning MacDonald knocked at his door, took in the calling tray, and went to prepare the King's bath. Twenty minutes later, hearing no sound of the familiar cough, he went back. The King seemed still to be asleep, so MacDonald went to bring a fresh tray. Still the King did not stir. His valet moved nearer, and found that he was dead. There was no sign of struggle and the bedclothes were not disturbed. For months the King had known that death might strike suddenly, in the midst of his State work, at his desk, during an audience, out in the woods—anywhere. So it was to Sandringham, where he was born, and where he spent the happiest hours of his life, that he came to die. This visit to Sandringham was a last-minute decision by the King. Did he have a premonition it would be his last? I think he did. Captain Sir Harold Campbell was Equerry-in-charge. It was he whom we roused with the sad news, and it was to him that fell the dreadful task of telling the Queen.

Never have I admired anyone as much as the Queen Mother on that day of sorrow. Pale and composed, hiding her tears, she was a source of strength to everyone, from Princess Margaret, quite overcome with grief, downward. No detail was too small for her attention. Early in the morning she sent for me. In the King's study she told me to arrange for a vigil to be kept by the deathbed.

"The King must not be left alone," she said.

A few hours later I saw her again on my way through the house. Now, dressed entirely in black (mourning clothes are always packed in the Royal luggage in case of the death of a Head of State or close relative), she was busy preparing food as she did every day for Crackers and Sue, the Royal Corgis. In her wisdom, the Queen knew that the carrying out of these ordinary little jobs of everyday life was the best anodyne for her sorrow. She tried to persuade Princess Margaret to follow her example, but though the Princess helped in writing some of the letters and cables that had to be dispatched, she did not seem to be able to stand up against the shock, and spent most of the time alone in her room. Between Princess Margaret and her father there was a special bond of love. In the King's eyes she could never do wrong. With his elder daughter consecrated to a lifetime of duty and responsibility, the King, we used to believe, felt that her sister should have every chance to enjoy life to the full, and would deny her nothing.

That night, and the next, after the embalmers from London had completed their task, MacDonald the valet, Hurle the chauffeur, Aubrey the Royal Chef, two police sergeants and I kept watch by the King's body. All of us were, as the Queen had asked, men whom the King had known personally. We kept up the vigil on both nights until six the following morning. On the evening of Friday, February 8, at 5 P.M., the King's body was placed in the coffin of Sandringham oak which estate carpenters had made. The wood came from the same tree as the coffin of his father, King George V, eighteen years earlier. James Emmerson, the estate carpenter, told me, with tears in his eyes, that he had been keeping the wood until Queen Mary died. We stood in darkness in the corridor outside the King's room, with the door open and the lights on inside so that we could see his face, calm and strangely unlined, in death.

Over at the church, estate workers, looking strange in their unfamiliar black clothes, came to take over the duty of watching over the coffin in the little church of St. Mary Magdalene at the estate gates.

Two strange incidents come to mind. Ever since the funeral of King Edward VII at Windsor, when the horses could not pull the gun carriage up the steep slope of Castle Hill, and bluejackets had to come to the rescue, there has been an almost morbid dread in the Royal Family of untoward incidents at funerals. The Imperial Crown falling off the coffin of George V as it was taken through the streets of London is another example. I was not, therefore, surprised when the officer commanding the detachment of Royal Horse Artillery ordered to Sandringham for the funeral told me he was determined to take extra precautions. His request, however, did surprise me. He asked for butter to put under the horses' hoofs, explaining that this would help to prevent them from slipping on the icy roads as they took the gun carriage down the hill to Wolferton Station en route for London. In those days, butter was still rationed at two ounces per person a week, and I thought it hard to have to rob my carefully guarded stores of ten or fifteen pounds to be trodden under horses' hoofs. So I demurred, and felt justified when the officer informed me later that he had telephoned for a supply of tallow fat to be sent from the R.H.A. headquarters at Regents Park.

By Queen Elizabeth's command, the body of the King remained in his bedroom, lying on his divan bed, his hands under the sheets, only his head visible, until the new Queen should come home, so that she might take her last look at her father. But when Queen Elizabeth II did arrive on Friday afternoon a few minutes before five o'clock, looking tired and pale after her flight from Africa, she thanked her mother—and declined. She felt, we were told, that she could not bear the strain of looking again at that dearly loved face which she had last seen smiling good-by to her when she entered the plane at London Airport only those few days before, to fly to Africa.

So the dead King was put in his coffin, and in the gathering dusk was wheeled, on the same estate handcart, with its noisy, iron-rimmed wheels, that had borne his father, King George V, and his grandmother, Queen Alexandra, on their last journeys, to the little church of St. Mary Magdalene. With his personal Piper, Pipe-Major Alec MacDonald, playing a Highland lament, and the pheasants joining in with their harsh calls from the adjoining park, the Queen, her mother, and sister, all in black and heavily veiled, walking behind with the Duke of Edinburgh, the King's body passed for the last time along the pleasant path through this parkland which he trod every Sunday when he was at Sandringham on his way to and from morning Church service. On top of the Royal coffin there were only three simple wreaths—from the Queen, the Queen Mother, and Princess Margaret.

Of the four Sovereigns of England, King George V, King George VI, King Edward VIII, and Queen Elizabeth II, under whom I had the honor to serve, it was King George VI whom I knew best as a man. I always had the greatest admiration for him. Unprepared for the throne, he took on the burden of being King when his elder brother, who had been trained for forty years to be King, laid it down. I suppose no King in history has ascended the throne in more difficult circumstances. Added to this was the King's personal distaste at that time for public ceremonies, and his speech impediment, which made public speaking a real ordeal for him.

Many times during his reign King George VI paid tribute to the aid, comfort, and support he had derived from his Queen, and those of us who knew him well, and who saw at close quarters what went on behind the scenes in Buckingham

Palace, know just how true this is. I often think that the British Monarchy owes a debt to Queen Elizabeth, the Queen Mother, which can never be fully paid. It was she who sustained and guided King George VI in those difficult early days on the throne. It was she who encouraged him to battle against and overcome the difficulty of his speech defect, and it was she who taught by her own example that public occasions should be happy occasions, and not ordeals.

Sometimes short-tempered and impatient, King George VI was a man who never bore a grudge for long. If he had been cross with one of his staff, he would afterward make amends, and there was no one in the Palace who was not delighted to do everything he or she could for the King. A happy sidelight on King George dates back to his first visit to Balmoral in the summer of 1937. The King was always deeply interested in youth and its welfare. The boys' camp which as Duke of York he had originated for boys from public schools, and from industry, was still functioning. That year he arranged for the camp, which had in previous years been held at Southwold in Suffolk, to be held at Abergeldie, about two miles from Balmoral Castle. Several times the King drove the Queen over to the camp, taking Princess Elizabeth and Princess Margaret with them, to join the boys at tea, and to sit with them round the campfire joining in the singing of their songs.

One day, I remember, the King, much to the delight of the boys, took a party of them out on the hills for a whole day's hike and climb. He wore shorts, an open-necked sports shirt with a pullover, and good stout ghillies shoes and carried, as he always did when he walked in the Highlands, his crummock. King George VI was, I think, never fitter in his life than at this time. He could walk at great speed on the moors—a feat which most people find very difficult because of the danger of putting one's foot in a clump of heather and catching it in a pothole or a rabbit hole. I have done this on many occasions with great pain to my ankles. But King George VI seemed to have an intuitive ability to walk literally without putting a foot wrong. Incidentally, this same ability used to serve him in good stead in the war days, when he could walk across muddy fields and come out on the other side with his shoes only slightly soiled, while those of everyone else in the party would be covered with mud. No one, neither the King himself nor any of those in close contact with him, seemed to know the secret of how he did it.

I believe he was quite proud of this ability, because if there was one thing he prided himself on, it was neatness of dress. King George VI was no lover of exaggeration in any direction, least of all in clothes, but his suits, though always cut on conservative lines, were models of excellent taste. His shirts and ties were chosen in quiet, blending tones, and it was only toward the end of his life that he let his sartorial imagination have rein, and designed himself the dinner jacket in Royal Stewart tartan which in his last few years was his almost invariable wear in the evenings at home.

But though conservative, he was most particular about his clothes. They had to be immaculate, and perfectly pressed. He wore his trousers with the ordinary creases in the center, not, as did his father, creased at the side, and he never succumbed to the fashion with men-about-town in the years just before the war of wearing trousers without turn-ups. His shoes were, of course, handmade by one of the best shoemakers in the world. He preferred heavy brogues to any other type of shoe, and wore these with every kind of suit, except formal morning wear. Cleaning these shoes, which were made either of blacking leather or tan calf, was quite a ritual. First they had to be brushed, and if necessary washed with leather soap until every particle of mud and dirt was removed from soles and heels as well as uppers. Then, when the leather was dry again, Tom Jerram or Jimmy MacDonald would carefully rub in a small quantity of wet blacking—the kind that Dickens helped to make when he was a boy in a London factory— or else a special dry blacking which had to be moistened preferably with spittle. Then came the boning—working hard at the leather with the polished leg bone of a deer, to force the blacking right into the leather. After many minutes of really hard work, a shine would begin to appear on the dull surface, and after a further five or ten minutes' work with the bone, finished off with a duster, the King's shoes would have a deep and lasting shine that you could literally see your face in. The King had always twenty or thirty pairs of shoes in his wardrobe, and it was his valet's job to see that there were always half a dozen pairs of brown and black ready for instant use.

He was as choosy about his country clothes as about town wear, and never, shooting in the coverts or walking round the farms at Windsor or Sandringham, would you see King George VI looking anything but well turned out. He abhorred slovenly dress, and any visitor arriving to see him not properly turned out could go away in the certainty that he had made a bad impression on his Sovereign.

In the war days, the King was most particular about his Service uniforms. He always made a point of being the best-turned-out officer at any parade or inspection he took, and his Sam Browne belt was reputed to have the highest gloss of any in the British Army. When General, now Field Marshal Lord, Montgomery waged his famous desert war leading his troops with a beret and somewhat un-regulation clothing, the King, admiring Monty as a warrior, could never bring himself to approve of his uniform. "Bad for discipline," he would mutter, when some new picture of the informal General ap-

peared in the Press. "I suppose he knows what he's doing!"
More to the King's taste was the attire of Monty's Com-
mander-in-Chief, General, now Field Marshal Lord, Alexander. A Guardsman, General Alexander shared the King's
views on parade equipment, whatever he may have worn on
the battlefield, and the only time the King ever saw a Sam
Browne and shoes with a polish to rival his own was when
he went into whatever field of operations, Southern Command,
Africa, Italy, or elsewhere, where General Alexander was in
charge.

The King's shirts were tailored for him, a dozen at a time,
and when he died, the wardrobe room at Buckingham Palace
was stacked with scores and scores of day shirts, sports shirts,
evening shirts, and others, many of them still unworn.

He disliked mackintoshes and raincoats, and never carried
an umbrella. For private wear in the country, he liked soft
felt hats with turn-down brims, for town wear or the races
(except for Ascot and Epsom, where top hats and morning
clothes were the order of the day) a bowler.

To return to Balmoral: he was tireless on the hills at Balmoral, as many of the Royal ghillies could testify. Often at
shooting parties he would walk his guests "off their feet"!
The boys from his camp were in good condition, too, and
when they and their Royal guide got back to camp that evening they were all in the best of spirits. Before the camp was
broken up the King and Queen gave a tea party for the boys
in the ballroom of Balmoral Castle. The fare was quite plain,
with good large cups of tea all round and great quantities of
bread and butter and fancy cakes. But the Royal Chef had
not thought of the healthy vigorous young appetites of the
boys, who had spent the last fortnight out in the open air on
the hills, but had cut his bread on a machine in the delicate
thin slices suitable for the Royal tea table. With a smile on his

face the King watched the boys picking up slice after slice, gliding it off their plates pancake-wise and eating it in one mouthful. The King sent a Page over to me with orders, and I went back into the kitchen to cut sandwich loaves into thick hunks by hand, just as I remember doing when I was a Boy Scout many years before. The thicker slices, liberally spread with fresh farmhouse butter, were much enjoyed by the boys.

The King laughed delightedly and afterward pulled his Chef's leg for misjudging the appetites of the boys.

I remember the Chef telling me afterward that the King had advised him to "go away and read Billy Bunter stories. That'll put you right for the next time." Unfortunately there never was to be a next time. That, though we did not know it, was the last of the Royal boys' camps before the war and after the war the King was never able to attend another camp. But he retained his interest in the movement that he had started and talked to his son-in-law, the Duke of Edinburgh, about it.

King George VI was essentially a family man. He found his greatest happiness with his wife and children, but he was also very devoted to the other members of his family, particularly to Queen Mary. For his brothers, too, the King had a great deal of affection, especially for the late Duke of Kent, whose sudden death on Active Service was a great blow to him. I remember that sad day in August, 1942. It was a very bad day at Balmoral, with the mountains veiled in mist and heavy rain falling, so heavy that the King could not go out shooting until very late in the morning.

The day passed slowly, and dinner was served as usual. The Pipers were playing after dinner when a telephone call came to the Castle switchboard from the Air Ministry. It was Sir Archibald Sinclair, the Air Minister, himself, asking to speak to the Private Secretary on duty, who happened to be Sir Eric Mieville, a close personal friend of King George VI and Queen

Elizabeth, as well as Assistant Private Secretary to the King. Sir Eric went to the telephone to hear from Sir Archibald the tragic news that the Duke of Kent had been killed in a plane crash on a lonely mountainside in Sutherlandshire. With a pale face Sir Eric hurried into the dining room to break the news to the King and Queen. "It was the worst job I can remember having to do," he said afterward.

The Royal dinner party broke up at once. The King was in a state of great distress. In the drawing room afterward the Queen tried to comfort him, though she herself was breaking down, for both she and her husband were very fond of the Duke of Kent, and the blow was so sudden and unexpected. What added to our grief was the fact that we had all been looking forward to seeing the Duke of Kent at Balmoral on the Friday of that week, when he was due to join the Royal party. A ball had been arranged for that evening, with several of the Duke's favorite reels. He was a very good dancer and looked well in a kilt. He always added to the gaiety of the Castle when he came on a visit.

Next morning the Master of the Household, Sir Piers Legh, and one of the guests, the Earl of Eldon, a great friend of the King, set off in a shooting brake from Balmoral to drive over to Dunrobin Castle, the home of the Duke of Sutherland, where the Duke's body had been taken. The King asked them to go over to make formal identification. When they came back they told the King of the details of the finding of the Duke's body. It had been a local farmer and his son out on the moors rounding up some of their sheep in the mist who heard the crash. They first heard the noise of the engines of an aircraft flying very low and circling. Then suddenly there was a crash with tremendous explosions. Visibility was only a few yards in any direction, but the farmer and his son, knowing the moorland well, took less than an hour to find the plane. It had broken up into pieces, and there were several bodies scattered in various directions on the mountainside. The farmer was able to identify the Duke by the silver identity badge which he always wore on his wrist. The King at once gave orders for a funeral service at St. George's Chapel, Windsor, and had arrangements made for the conveyance of his beloved brother's body south. The King and Queen traveled down to Windsor in the Royal train from Balmoral for the funeral. When they came back, the King's first thought was to go and visit the scene of the crash. He was driven across the Highlands to Sutherlandshire and taken to the very spot where the plane had crashed. Loose pieces of wreckage still lay around in the heather in mute testimony to the death of that gallant young Prince, the first member of the Royal Family for many, many years to be killed on Active Service. The Duke was indeed on Active Service, for he was flying to Iceland for the Royal Air Force, in which he was a serving officer in the Welfare section.

Always thoughtful of others, even in the midst of his own sorrow, the King, after standing in silence for some time on the hillside looking at the remains of the plane, asked that the farmer and his son should be brought to him. He thanked them warmly for their prompt help and their good work in almost impossible conditions, and congratulated them on the way they had handled what must have been an appalling situation for them. By the King's orders a little stone cairn was erected on the exact spot in the heather where the Duke was found. Several times when the Duchess of Kent has been staying at Birkhall she has driven over to visit the spot. On these occasions the Duchess has driven alone. Just near the cairn the chauffeur has stopped the car and left the Duchess to walk the remaining few yards to stand alone with her thoughts at the place where her husband was killed.

The death of the Duke was one of the greatest shocks King George VI sustained throughout his life. His younger brother was such an eager young man, with a great zest for life and a wonderful future before him, married as he was to the lovely Princess Marina and father of three delightful children, the youngest of them being only a few months old at the time of his father's death.

The Duke of Kent was the most athletic-minded of all the Royal brothers. I had known him many times, when he was living either at his own house at Coppins at Iver or at his London home in Belgrave Square, telephone to the Metropolitan Police Officer who was permanently attached to his staff, and ask him to join him at Windsor before breakfast for a run. This run of six miles was one of the Duke's greatest pleasures, and I remember the large breakfasts he used to eat when he came in from one of these runs. The police officer, who is now in charge of one of the biggest Divisions of the metropolis, was by way of being a personal friend of the Duke's as well as his police officer. It was only because of a last-minute thought of the late Duke of Kent's that this man was saved from being killed in the crash with the Duke. At Invergordon, just before the take-off, the Duke told him not to accompany him, but to return to London, go to Coppins, and take the Duchess of Kent to Sandringham. It was at Crewe Station on his way back to London that the policeman learned of the terrible tragedy. It was a wheel-tapper on the railway who told him casually, " 'Ave you heard, chum? The Duke of Kent's dead!"

Watching the development and growth of Princess Elizabeth and Princess Margaret was one of the greatest of joys to King George VI. There was nothing he would not do to make his daughters happy. In the latter years of his life, when he knew, though he concealed the fact from everyone, that his life could not last very much longer, he took a more and more active interest in training Princess Elizabeth for the tremendous responsibilities which would one day be hers. I have heard many stories of the difficulties that existed between Queen Victoria and King Edward VII. There were servants at Buckingham Palace when I first went there who remembered vividly those days and could tell many tales of the disagreements between the Queen and her son. I have heard, too, of the difficulties that existed between King George V and the Duke of Windsor when he was Prince of Wales. I have had personal experience of some of these, and have seen the Prince of Wales, as he was then, come away from an interview with his father at which he had been reprimanded for exposing himself to danger when he used to ride at point-to-point meetings. His face would be white with anger, and he would leave the Palace without a word.

I do not think any Sovereign of England has been taught so much in advance about his work by his predecessor as Queen Elizabeth II was by her father. It was always a joy to see them together, so happy in each other's company. The King liked to join in his daughters' amusements, particularly in their dancing. King George VI himself was a very good dancer and delighted in private dances, though he disliked very much large public dances and charity balls. In the latter part of the war, when the danger of bombing had temporarily ceased, the King used to give a small dance once a fortnight at Buckingham Palace. It would be held in the Bow Room on the ground floor of the Palace. Young officers from the Guards and other regiments would be invited as partners for the Princesses and some of their young women friends. It was a very happy family affair, at which the King and the Queen always joined in the dances. I remember one evening seeing the King leading a conga line, followed by the Queen, Princess Elizabeth, Princess Margaret, their partners, and their guests. The King, in a dinner jacket and black tie, was thoroughly enjoying himself, laughing aloud as he led his guests this way and that way through the maze of corridors of the Palace. For some time the dance band was playing to a completely empty room, but they continued with the "Hi-Hi Conga" tune until eventually the line of dancers returned with the King, a little out of breath, leading them back to the room. This was the Royal Family in private enjoyment. It would have done millions of the King's subjects good to see the simple pleasures in which they delighted.

King George VI's predecessor, King Edward VIII, was quite different from either his father or his brother—so much so that I am devoting a separate chapter to his reign and personality. Kings George V and VI were much of a pattern, though the son lacked the father's austerity and authoritative manner. Yet both were essentially the same in their values and philosophies of life. Both were primarily family men, though the elder George's relationships with his sons and daughters were never quite, I felt, as close as were those of King George VI with Princess Elizabeth and Princess Margaret. George V was a kindly man, with a warm heart, which he seemed to think it was unfitting for a King to reveal, so he took elaborate care to conceal his real feelings, at any rate to his staff, both official and Household. His bearded face, with its look of unquestionable authority, and his deep, resonant voice were rather frightening when you met him for the first time. He never took any steps to put newcomers at their ease. In those days the distance between the Sovereign and even his closest relatives was something that had to be maintained all the time. This was undoubtedly a barrier to that complete understanding which existed between King George V's second son and his daughters.

It was for his own sister, the Princess Victoria, that King George V had the greatest affection. It was well known at Buckingham Palace that King George V always spent a quarter of an hour every morning, no matter where he was—London, Sandringham, Windsor, Cowes, or Balmoral—telephoning his sister, telling her his latest family news and discussing affairs of the day with her. When in December, 1935, shortly after the wedding of the Duke and Duchess of Gloucester, the King was told the sad news that Princess Victoria had died at Coppins, her house at Iver (which she bequeathed to the late Duke of Kent), it was a great blow to him. From that day he seemed to lose much of his zest for life. I remember his valet, Mr. Richard Howlett, coming to me afterward to tell me that he was very concerned at the change in the King. The death of his favorite sister had been a grievous blow to him, from which, as it transpired, he was never to recover.

King George V spent many of his happiest days at Sandringham and Balmoral. He was one of the finest shots in the country in his prime with a double-barreled sporting gun and with a sporting rifle. The King was never very fond of fishing, but on one occasion he went out with Queen Mary and the Castle guests on a special expedition to Loch Muick, where trout abounded. Ghillies and keepers went with the Royal party, and soon all of them, with the King and his guests, were fishing for trout. There was a wonderful catch, and the King and his Chef, who had been driven out from the Castle with an assistant to bring flour, cooking fat, and a frying pan, proceeded to fry the trout over a wood fire. It was delightful to see the King enjoying the trout fresh from the water.

The Chef on this picnic was Monsieur Cedard, who had been with the King ever since the Delhi Durbar of 1911. There was an old association between them. Cedard knew exactly what the King liked, and the King trusted his Chef implicitly. Cedard was taken ill a few weeks later and died, a sad blow for the King. He was always most distressed when the familiar face of one of his old retainers disappeared for-ever from the circle at Buckingham Palace. I remember an-other occasion at Cowes, when aboard the Royal yacht *Victoria and Albert,* one of the Pages of the Presence, a dear old fellow—Thomas Snowden—was taken ill and died quite suddenly. When the news was broken to King George V he was very distressed. "Poor Snowden! poor Snowden!" he said; "he had been with me for a long time. There are not many like him nowadays." Tommy Snowden would have been proud to have known of this tribute.

For the last few years of his life, unknown to the public, King George V's health was a matter of constant concern to Queen Mary and the Royal physicians. At the beginning of Jubilee year, 1935, it was arranged for the King to go down to Compton Place, the Duke of Devonshire's home at East-bourne, for a period of rest and recuperation. So limited was the accommodation at Compton Place that many of the staff had to be boarded out in a school. It was Queen Mary who made these arrangements, and it was typical of her care and thought that before we were installed in the schoolhouse, she went there to inspect it.

One of my friends on the staff, more fortunate than I, had a bedroom in Compton House itself, immediately above the one occupied by King George V. Every evening after our duties were over we went for a walk along the front. It was sometimes midnight when we returned. One morning I met my friend just before breakfast and noticed that he seemed very worried. When I asked him what was the trouble, he told me that the King had sent his nurse, Sister Black, to find out who it was in the room above who made so much noise coming in late at night. My friend was distressed to think of the annoyance he had caused the King. Later that day, however, Sister Black, that devoted woman who nursed King George V from the time of his serious illness in 1928 right up to his death, came to my friend to tell him that the King had laughed when informed of the identity of the culprit. She told him that the King had suggested that it might be a good idea for him to remove his shoes on the staircase and carry them up to his room whenever he came in late! This he did for the remainder of the visit.

The last sight I had of King George V was at Sandringham in his last Christmas there. It was in 1935, when the fourteen-hole private golf course still existed. A few days after Christmas I was walking down No. 1 fairway, after having driven off in a friendly match, when out of the mist came the King, mounted on his white pony, Jock. Walking by the head of the pony, as if leading it along, was the little figure of Princess Elizabeth. She was taking her grandfather back to the house along the pathway that runs through the golf course. I had not seen the King for some days, and it was a shock to me to notice such a sudden change in his appearance. I was certain then that I was looking at a man who had not much longer to live.

The Christmas festivities went on as usual, and soon after the beginning of the New Year I left Sandringham to return to London to make preparations for another visit to Compton Place, where the King was to spend a month. His doctors were convinced that the sea air had done him a great deal of good. But I had been back in Buckingham Palace only a day or two when we heard from Sandringham that the King had taken to his bed. This was at midday on a Thursday. The King's doctors came to Buckingham Palace for a consultation before going off to Sandringham. The Palace was indeed a gloomy place that day, for it was empty except for the Duke of Gloucester confined to his room with a septic throat. The arrangements for the Eastbourne visit were at once canceled, and the King grew steadily worse. When we heard at the Palace that the Archbishop of Canterbury and the heart specialist, Sir Maurice Cassidy, had gone to Sandringham we knew that the end was near.

On Monday, January 20, which was to be the King's last day on earth, all the members of the Royal Family had gathered at Sandringham, the Prince of Wales flying there with the Duke of York; only the Duke of Gloucester, still ill, remaining in London. I remember the feeling of shock with which I watched a Royal Standard being packed at Buckingham Palace to be taken to Sandringham to wrap round the King's coffin. It was much more than just losing a master— even to us it seemed that it was the end of an epoch; and I can remember that night the terrible feeling of gloom and desolation that spread, not only among us all at Buckingham Palace, but everywhere. It was exactly midnight when my telephone rang and the Palace operator gave me the news, just received from Sandringham, that the King had died five minutes earlier. The servants who had been in personal attendance on King George V were heartbroken at his death. They had really loved their Royal master. I remember the late King's Page coming down to my office as soon as the Court had returned from Sandringham. He looked most upset, bewildered, and lost. There were tears in his eyes when he told me that although the end did not come until nearly midnight on the Monday, he had known that the King could not last much longer on the Friday evening. On that night, for the first time in the Page's long experience of King George V, he refused to eat his oysters.

"I knew there was something dreadfully wrong," said the old servant. "He'd never done that before."

Indeed, during the last two days of his life, the only nourishment that passed King George V's lips were raw eggs and brandy beaten up together by the French Pastry Cook and served in small doses at frequent intervals on the doctor's orders.

So passed a great man and a great King, and so ended the really spacious days of the British Monarchy, as I had known them in my time at the Palace and the other Royal houses.

If there were differences between the Kings whom I served under, there were also great differences between the three Queens, Queen Mary and Queen Elizabeth, Queens Consort, and Her Majesty Queen Elizabeth II, the Queen Regnant.

Queen Mary was a remote, unapproachable figure to those beneath her station in life. At least that was the superficial impression she gave. She never for one second relaxed control. Her figure was always erect, her walk one of dignity, her eyes were always looking into the future. She was indeed a majestic figure, and it was with a sense of awe that one approached her presence.

Queen Elizabeth, the Queen Mother now, in her days as Queen Consort was a much more approachable person. Of course, any attempt to take advantage of proximity to the Queen or any momentary forgetfulness of the respect due to her were quickly rewarded with an icy stare from those beautiful blue eyes which at other times could look in such a friendly way at the world. But in the ordinary way Queen Elizabeth was much easier to talk to and much more understanding, it seemed, of the trials and troubles of other people's lives than was the case with Queen Mary. Actually, it was probably the shyness that was an inherited characteristic of Queen Mary that prevented her from being on easy terms with members of her staff, except those who were in close personal attendance upon her. From people who knew her really well I often heard that she was, beneath this icy regal surface, a warmhearted, very friendly, and sympathetic human being. But she certainly gave all of us the impression of aloof severity, except in times of trouble, when she would always do everything she could to help anyone on her staff whose misfortunes came to her ears.

With King George V, Queen Mary made an ideal Consort. They had many tastes in common, and one of the foundations of their mutual happiness was, I always thought, their mutual regard for time. King George V was the most punctual of men, as I have indicated elsewhere in these pages. Only second to him perhaps as a timekeeper was Queen Mary. I can recall no occasion all through the years I saw them together when Queen Mary ever kept King George V waiting for a minute.

Queen Elizabeth as Consort was an ideal helpmate for King George VI. He looked up to her in countless ways and relied on her implicitly for support and aid in his great task. But there was one bone of contention frequently between them. King George VI, with the same naval training as his father, had almost as equally high regard for the value of exact punctuality. Queen Elizabeth, on the other hand, though she was never unpunctual intentionally, would very often, particularly on Royal tours in the provinces, find herself engaged in conversation with someone and become so interested in the talk that she momentarily forgot time, with the result that on many occasions the Royal program was thrown slightly out of schedule and the King was kept waiting. But King George VI grew to know this little habit of his wife's and on most occasions used to greet her rather tardy appearance with a smile and an understanding look.

Of course, those stories about Queens going into the Palace kitchens to prepare meals and take a personal part in the domestic side of Palace life are just fairy tales. Actually, a Queen is always too busy with much more important affairs to have time, let alone inclination, to meddle with the domestic running of the Palace.

But both Queen Mary and Queen Elizabeth always made it a point, as does the present Queen, of keeping a degree of personal control over the activities of the staff, of seeing, for example, the daily menus for themselves. The Palace arrangements are such that in ordinary times the daily routine can continue week in and week out without any guidance or word from the Queen. But when there are special events ahead, a State visit or some guests whom the King and Queen want to honor specially, or anything out of the ordinary, then, in the days of King George VI, Queen Elizabeth would herself send for the actual members of the Household staff concerned with the new arrangements and give them verbal instructions with her own lips.

In the days of King George V, Queen Mary rarely, if ever, did this. Instead, she would give her orders to her lady-in-waiting or to her personal Page, and they in turn would transmit the Queen's wishes to the people actually concerned. It was all part of the greater separation of Royalty in those days.

Today the process of familiarization between the members of the Royal Family and their personal staff has gone much further, and it is no uncommon thing at Buckingham Palace for the Queen to give orders personally to one of her lower servants or for the Duke of Edinburgh to pick up the telephone and casually indicate his wishes for the day to whoever is responsible for making those arrangements.

But even Queen Mary could unbend on occasion, particularly when the Court was in the Highlands. As I have said, I always found that north of the Tweed members of the Royal Family seemed to become much more human and approachable than ever they were in the south. This was certainly the case with Queen Mary.

In her days as Queen Consort it was no unusual sight to see her familiar green Daimler pull up outside a tiny cottage a few miles from Balmoral Castle on a Saturday or Sunday afternoon. The Queen would get out and examine with her well-informed eye the flowers growing outside the cottage windows, before going herself and knocking with her own hand on the door.

Always she asked, "Please may I come in?" And always, of course, the loyal Scottish inhabitants were delighted to welcome their Queen into their humble homes.

I remember once being myself on a visit to some of the Royal tenants when the green car pulled up outside.

"It's the Queen," said my host. "Thank guidness we've the best tea service out."

A moment or two later there came a knock on the door and in came Queen Mary with her lady-in-waiting. She sat down and was soon chatting away to my host and hostess, just as though this was an ordinary afternoon call for her—I was going to write just as though she had known them all her life. In fact, she had known them, as she had known all the tenants on the Royal estate by name for many years. With her remarkable memory she could always recall how many children a couple had, what were their names, what they were doing when she last heard of them, and so on.

As I sat there on that Saturday afternoon, it amazed me to see how the Queen's mind worked. She was so alert. Her eyes seemed to take in the whole room so quickly and she noted every detail.

On the table, which had already been set for tea when I arrived, the Queen noticed some jam in a dish.

"That's homemade, I'm sure," said the Queen. It was, and she asked in a most understanding way about the recipe, as though she had made jam many times. In fact, Queen Mary did not make jam, even at Sandringham, but she liked to be well informed about all that went on.

Her knowledge of pictures, furniture, ornaments, and antiques in general frequently staggered people who did not realize that she was indeed an expert, particularly on Georgian silverware and Georgian furniture. Buckingham Palace as it is arranged today, with the period furniture in tasteful order, owes much to Queen Mary. I was told that it was she who, when she first went to Buckingham Palace, back in 1911, began a gigantic spring cleaning operation in which all sorts of rubbish accumulated over the years was got rid of and valuable and beautiful pieces of furniture that had been hidden away in the storerooms were brought out and arranged in their appropriate periods.

She was one of the most thoughtful of women. I remember when she came to Sandringham for the first Christmas of the new reign after the accession of King George VI, she brought her own staff with her from Marlborough House so as not to add any strain to the staff fully engaged in looking after the King and Queen and their guests. With her she brought her own Page and footman, her own two dressers and a housemaid, as well as her chauffeur and car washer to look after her green Daimler.

Queen Mary loved Sandringham. While her husband was on the throne, she never went to their Norfolk home except at Christmas time and knew it only in the rather dark and foggy days of December, January, and February. When she had become Queen Mother, Queen Mary decided that she would like to go to Sandringham in the summer. King George VI at once put his Norfolk home at her disposal whenever she wanted it, and from then on she went to Norfolk for her summer holiday, August after August, glorying in the summer beauty of the Sandringham countryside with its masses of rhododendrons and lovely other blossoms. The Chinese winter garden at Sandringham was Queen Mary's pet. She had originated it in her young days as Queen, and right to the days of her last visit to Sandringham she spent many happy hours there.

Another example of Queen Mary's methodical mind which I recall is the way she always had the empty boxes in which her son, King George VI, sent her grouse from Balmoral returned to us at the Castle. Many a lesser person conveniently "forgot" to send these boxes back, much to the annoyance of the gamekeepers at Balmoral. But Queen Mary never lost one.

When Queen Elizabeth came to the throne with her husband King George VI, her greatest interest naturally centered on her two children, Princess Elizabeth and Princess Margaret. We at Buckingham Palace, who already knew the two Princesses as delightful afternoon visitors when they would come across from 145 Piccadilly to cheer up their grandfather, King George V, were very glad at the thought of having a nursery at the Palace and children running about the corridors. The Royal children soon made themselves at home in the Palace. They were given nursery quarters on the second floor of the northwest corner of the Palace, adjoining the rooms where the Royal dressers and valets had their apartments. These are the rooms which are today occupied by Prince Charles and Princess Anne.

The coming of the children meant several changes in routine, especially in the way of meals. There was a special nursery menu with printed forms for each day of the week.

On these forms the Chef would write in his suggestions for the day's meals, and they would be sent up to the Queen or to the head Nannie, Mrs. Knight. Sometimes, when the Queen thought that her children should have special food, she would herself write in her orders for the day. One order we had direct from the Queen was to make sure we always had a good stock of fresh oranges. We were never allowed to run out of this fruit, whatever the season of the year, because several decanters of pure orange juice had to be sent up to the nursery during the course of each day. Queen Elizabeth II also believes in the value of fresh fruit juices for her children.

One little example I may give of what I call Queen Elizabeth's approachability. At the end of the war the Queen wanted to thank members of the women's staff at Buckingham Palace and the wives of the men who had been busy knitting woolen comforts for the Queen to send to the troops during the war years.

"I shall give them a party myself," declared the Queen, and orders to this effect were passed down to us. This was one of the first of the postwar afternoon tea parties given at the Palace, and the Royal gesture was much appreciated by the women who had worked for her.

Queen Elizabeth II as a reigning Queen falls into an entirely different category from her mother or her grandmother. Most of her time at Buckingham Palace is naturally occupied with those many affairs of State which demand the Sovereign's personal attention. Few people outside the Royal Household and the Royal staff have any realization of the immense amount of paper work which the Sovereign is called upon to deal with wherever he or she may be. Even at Balmoral and at Sandringham the famous "boxes" (actually steel-lined, red-covered dispatch cases in which are contained Cabinet memoranda and other documents of State importance) follow the

Sovereign. There is a daily private aeroplane service operated by the Queen's Flight, to bring the boxes from London, and to take them back when the Queen has read, signed, or approved the papers in them. There is little time for the Queen to devote to the domestic side of the Palace, or even to her own private family life. It is for this reason that whenever she can get away from Buckingham Palace to the quiet peace of Windsor Castle, where she has her private apartments arranged as a flat within the Castle, or to Sandringham, she likes to be alone with her husband and children, but she is still not free from State documents.

The Queen thoroughly enjoys her work. Anyone who has spent any time close to her knows that, and knows, too, that this is the secret of her happiness, and of that wonderful control and calmness which she displays when other folk round her are getting ruffled by some minor or major crisis. This does not mean that the Queen never gets angry. She does. I know, because on one occasion I had the very unpleasant experience of being the unwitting cause of her displeasure. It was during the Balmoral visit of 1952, after the Coronation, that Group Captain Peter Townsend, then Acting Master of the Household, sent for me to tell me the Queen wanted me to send out invitations for a ball she was giving at the Castle that evening. I had my hands pretty full, as I was running the whole of the belowstairs part of the Castle. Usually, for these private dances, we had three or four days' notice. This time we had to do the whole thing in a hurry, and tackled the task with a will. By steady hard work we got through the longish list of people to whom the Queen wanted cards to be sent, and the invitations in her name had been written out and taken round by motorcycle by one of the Balmoral estate workers to be delivered by hand to people like Lord Glentaner, the Farquharsons at Braemar Castle, the Queen's domestic chaplain, the apothecary at Ballater, and a few old retainers dwelling in scattered cottages around the Castle.

When the time for the ball to start at nine-thirty arrived I was congratulating myself that everything had been well done, and anticipating, perhaps, a word of thanks or pleasure from the Queen. All seemed in order. The Scottish band, led by Mrs. Milne, a middle-aged lady from the nearby village of Kincardine, nearly always chosen to play at these less formal dances, had arrived in good time, and were ready—pianist, saxophonist, and drummer—to begin the program. In the Royal dining room and the staff mess I saw that the tables were nicely laid out with glasses, china, cutlery, and refreshments. A few minutes later the Queen and the Duke of Edinburgh led their guests down the staircase to the ballroom, and I decided that I had earned a rest and a glass of whisky with one or two of my colleagues in my own quarters.

I had been sitting there for about fifteen minutes when there was a knock on the door and a footman told me, "The Group Captain wants you at once." I went to the ballroom at once. I picked out the Group Captain, and made my way toward him. As I drew near to the Royal dais where Group Captain Townsend stood, I chanced to pass close by the Queen, and immediately knew my presentiments were right. Instead of the smile of welcome she usually bestowed on me, I received a look of displeasure. Her lips were pursed, and she said nothing at all. Still unconscious of having done anything wrong, I heard Group Captain Townsend say, "The Queen is furious with you. Why was not Elizabeth M—— invited to the ball, when I told you this morning to do so?"

So that was it. All my extra work counted for nothing against the fact that I had omitted to send an invitation to a former housemaid whom the Queen wanted to be present at the ball. Of course it was a bad slip, and I was very sorry, especially for the maid in question. However, I should have known. In my years on the Royal staff I found that mistakes are *not* permitted. You can do your job well and to everyone's satisfaction for year after year, and never hear anything. Then, one mistake, and you are in bad favor, likely to stay that way for a long time and be remembered as "the man who forgot to send out the proper invitation."

In her days as Princess Elizabeth, the Queen was taught to shoot by McHardie, her father's head stalker, who had known her ever since her days as a tiny girl. He was always delighted to take her out for a day's stalking on the mountains. The Princess on these occasions would dress in long plus-four trousers, heavy boots, and a sweater, with a scarf tied round her head. She would stalk her stag like any man, crawling on all fours or lying flat down on the wet grass among the boulders to get her chance at a shot. She would never give up until she had either killed her animal or had at least three chances at him. Actually she rarely missed with her first shot, and I have known her to kill two, three, and once four stags in a single day's stalking. McHardie, a stern judge if ever there was one, and a man not given to undue praise, gave me this verdict on the Princess after one long day out with her. "She shoots very well indeed. She is a good wee lassie," said McHardie. Since she has been on the throne, Queen Elizabeth has given up stalking.

It was at Balmoral in 1946 that we first realized that the Princess had found romance. An unexpected visitor to the Royal party whose name had not been included in the advance lists turned out to be the handsome young Prince Philip of Greece and Denmark. Most of us knew already that it was to Prince Philip that the Princess had been writing, almost daily, for many months past, and we all knew, too, that his photograph, showing him in naval uniform with a beard, stood in a prominent place in a silver frame upon her desk. So everyone at the Castle was anxious to see him and find out for himself what kind of man it was who had won the heart of our dearly beloved Princess. Prince Philip went out with the guns as soon as he arrived at the Castle, but he had not had much chance to practice shooting in those days. The ghillies and the stalkers, talking over his performance at the butts in the evenings as they took their whisky in the Staff Canteen, were not very enthusiastic. They declared him in those days to be a poor shot and rather erratic.

It is a tribute to him that the same men who summed him up in that way in 1946 now have high praise for him as a shot. In this, as in so many other directions, Prince Philip has shown that when he makes up his mind to do a thing, he will do it as well as anyone else, and better than most. In my last few months at Buckingham Palace I found that Prince Philip (as we all continued to know him) was gradually taking in many ways the place of his father-in-law. But the Duke of Edinburgh knows very well that it is his job to help his Queen in her domestic affairs, and he therefore takes a keen personal interest in every detail of the ways the Palace and the other Royal households are run.

I remember one of the Senior Pages, a man who spent most of his life in the Royal service, coming in to see me one evening not long before I left the Palace to tell me how sad it made him to see the Duke of Edinburgh sitting in the King's place and taking his chair in the Royal dining room at Windsor Castle when the Queen and the Duke were there for the Ascot summer meeting.

But I told him changes must come. I am sure that King George VI, if he is able to know what is going on in the Royal Family which he headed so long, must feel great contentment at the way that his son-in-law has taken over so many of the duties inseparable from the throne and thus allowed his daughter to devote all her energies to her tremendous task of ruling over the British Commonwealth.

Between the Accession and the Coronation there was a period of great uncertainty and concern at Buckingham Palace. So to everyone in the Palace Coronation Day came as something of a relief. It marked the real beginning of the new reign. Now it was plain sailing again. The Palace staff paused to take account of the changes the new Queen had brought with her. Before she came from Clarence House, her home as Princess, there had been a good deal of nervousness, as when King Edward VIII came over. Tales had reached us of the decidedly different way they had of doing things "across the road." Many of the older folk prophesied sweeping changes once more, the end of the old regime, and a completely "new deal" for the Palace. People trembled for their jobs, and when "P.P."—as Prince Philip, the Duke of Edinburgh, is always known among his friends and staff—began a tour of inspection of every department within a couple of days of his arrival at the Palace, the prophecies seemed justified.

The Duke is nothing if not thorough. He went into every one of the four hundred odd rooms in the Palace, and asked, I think, nearly every one of the men and women on the staff exactly what he or she was doing, and why. One point that baffled the Duke at first, I recall, was our system of meals. He could not understand why it was necessary to have two services of lunch in both the Servants' Hall and the Steward's Room (where the senior servants eat), nor why other servants were needed to wait on them. The system of days on and off, by which menservants work from 6 A.M. till 11 P.M. or later, and take the next day off, also puzzled him. When it was pointed out to him that there must always be servants on duty, so their meals and hours must be "staggered," the Duke suggested introducing a cafeteria system.

The mechanics of the Palace seemed to fascinate him. He wanted to know how everything worked, why this particular method was used, and some of the questions he asked were exactly those which lots of us had wanted to ask for years. Time-wasting is an infuriation to the Duke. He likes to get things done quickly as well as efficiently. When he found that to transmit a simple order from the Queen or himself it took about four men to pass it on to the right person, he decided something must be done. Instead, for example, of sending for his secretary or an equerry and asking him to tell the Page on duty to tell the Comptroller of Supply to arrange for sandwiches to be left for him at night, he would send down a scribbled note in pencil direct, stating his requirements. Or the telephone in the Royal Mews or the Chef's office would ring—and the surprised chauffeur or cook would recognize the Duke's voice, giving his orders personally.

"Prince Philip's trying to run the Palace like H.M.S. *Magpie*" (the frigate he commanded in the Mediterranean), was a comment I often heard.

And he was, indeed, impatient of many of our ways. The Duke is a man of very alert perception, with trained eyes that miss no more when he is walking round Buckingham Palace than they did when he made a captain's inspection aboard *Magpie*. In the tradition of his uncle, Admiral Earl Mountbatten, whom, more than any man, he takes as his model for life, Prince Philip told his crew in *Magpie* that he wanted them to help him make her the smartest, most efficient ship in the Mediterranean Fleet.

He could not tell us exactly that at the Palace, but he left no doubt in anyone's mind that he wanted the Palace to be run with maximum efficiency, and intended to see that it was. You may think it strange that it was the husband, and not his Royal wife, who took the greatest interest in this side of affairs, but the Queen, of course, was—and still is to this day —so occupied with the great affairs of State that she has no time to spare for the detailed side of running her home. Running the Palace, and overhauling its complex machinery, too, gave Prince Philip a job of his own, and an outlet for his very active temperament.

Nothing escapes him. At Sandringham, where the Queen and the Duke with the children and other members of the Royal Family had gone for their first Christmas, I was waiting one day in a small room near the big front door to catch the doctor, Dr. Ansell (the same one whose sad job it had been to certify the King's death), as he came from his daily call, to ask him to attend one of my staff. As I waited, the door opened, and the Duke of Edinburgh's fair head appeared. He was on one of his "finding-out" missions. I stood up and bowed. He smiled, and went out. About an hour later I was back in my office, having seen the doctor, and looked up from my papers as the door opened. Again it was the Duke.

"What?" said the Duke. "You here? Do you have two offices?"

"No, sir," I replied, and explained that I had been waiting to see the doctor.

"I see," said Prince Philip. " I just wanted to know."

Then, pulling aside a curtain at the end of the room, he asked, "And what goes on here?"

I told him that was where I took my meals—and laughed as I saw him spot a bottle of orangeade on the table, laid for my luncheon. Actually it was for my small son, who with his mother was staying in the nearby village, coming in to lunch with me each day by the Queen's permission. The bottle of beer for me had not yet made its appearance.

In the kitchens the Duke's curiosity was insatiable. At the Palace and at Sandringham he would suddenly appear and ask anyone who happened to be on duty what the various fittings and equipment were for. The kitchens at the Palace are rather old-fashioned in appearance, though they were redecorated and altered considerably toward the end of King George VI's reign. They are designed on the grand scale, as they need to be. Not only are the small meals for the Royal Family themselves all cooked here, as well as those for the Royal Household, but also when there is a big dinner party or other function, all the food is cooked here—four or five courses for two hundred or more guests, if it is a State banquet. It took some time to persuade the Duke that all the masses of gleaming copper pans, and the scores of other kitchen fittings, were really needed.

The kitchens are on the ground floor on the south of the building, the Royal dining room on the northeast corner, on the first floor, a distance of about a quarter of a mile or so for the food to be carried from the oven to the table. Every Monarch in turn coming to Buckingham Palace in modern times has tried to alter the kitchens. King George VI installed a hot plate and an electric grill in the anteroom by the side of the dining room, where some dishes could be kept hot, and others, like the chafing-dish recipes that were among his favorites, cooked on the spot. But the Duke thought the whole kitchen should be moved and rebuilt directly under the dining room, so that there could be a direct lift service almost from oven to table. It was, of course, a sound idea, typical of the Duke's practical mind, but we knew it would not be put into effect. Similar schemes had been put forward in the past, but all had been abandoned. So was the Duke's. There was nothing wrong with his plan so far as construction work was concerned, but the cost was prohibitive.

"I would like to see the figures to prove it," said the Duke. The accountants headed by the Keeper of the Privy Purse, and their opposite numbers at the Ministry of Works, set about estimating the cost of the move. It ran into over £30,000, and the Duke dropped the scheme.

Another idea he had was for setting up a laundry in the Palace, to save the outside laundry bill, which costs many hundreds of pounds a year. This, too, we knew as an old idea —indeed, many years ago all the washing and ironing were done within the Palace, and only after very careful checking of prices and costs and other details, was the contract placed with an outside firm. The same applied to another of his plans for ceasing to buy bread and rolls outside and to set up a bakery in the Palace instead. But it was no use telling the Duke about the past. He wanted to know what the position was today, and again the accountants got out their figures for wages, materials, and so on. Once more the Duke accepted the facts, and withdrew his plan—though not, I felt, without a certain amount of disappointment and regret. It seemed he would be much happier with all these things being done on the spot, where he could control them himself.

We heard no more about the laundry or the bakery, but the kitchen move was something the Duke was determined to push through. Eventually, though the main kitchens were left in place, the Duke's idea was partly adopted, and a new, completely modern kitchen, equipped with the very latest devices for using both electricity and gas (even in her own house the Queen has to display impartiality between the two nationalized industries), is now installed hard by the Royal dining room purely for preparing the family meals. The most unusual feature of the new kitchen is a "broche," or automatically turning gas spit, on which chicken or other poultry can be cooked as well as steaks. Under the turnspit there is a shallow trough which catches the grease or hot butter from whatever is being cooked, to allow the chef to baste the food continually. This is, according to the gastronomic experts, probably the best method of cooking poultry, and it is certainly one of the Queen's favorites. It was partly to enable him to learn all he could about this particular method, used more in France than in England, that the Queen sent her Chef, Ronald Aubrey, to Paris for lessons by some of the great chefs there while she was away on her Commonwealth tour in 1954.

Small things as well as big attracted the Duke's notice. Outside the kitchen larder at Sandringham one morning he saw the usual array of blocks of ice, newly brought in from King's Lynn, standing on the floor awaiting removal for use when required.

"That won't do," said the Duke.

He wanted a bench made for the ice to be stacked on, and that afternoon the estate carpenters, under Bob Marrington, the tapissier, were busy making and setting up the bench. Two days later the Duke came round again to see if his orders had been carried out, and was delighted to find the ice stacked on the newly fitted bench. What difference it made, none of us could discover, but the Duke was satisfied. The Queen, whenever she could spare the time, went into details of everything with her husband, but in general she left it to his judgment, and generally backed up any of his ideas.

For the first few months of their stay at the Palace, the Queen and the Duke used the Belgian Suite on the ground floor, at the back northwest corner of the building, eating in the Caernarvon Room, a large, high-ceilinged apartment, which has heard more of the secret history of the war than probably any other room in the world. For, as already stated, it was here that the late King used to lunch every Tuesday during the war with his Prime Minister, Mr. Winston Churchill. Later on the Queen and the Duke moved to the apartments they occupy today, the same suite on the first floor which King George VI and his father and grandfather before him used as their private quarters. Before they could do this, the Queen Mother had to sort out all her belongings, and arrange for their removal to Clarence House. It was a sad task for her. Gradually her rooms and the King's were emptied, though the work of sorting out the King's wardrobe and uniforms was so difficult that his valet, Mr. Tom Jerram, was still on it two years after his death.

One thing on which the Queen Mother insisted was the removal of the fireplace from her bedroom. This was a magnificent one of white marble, given her as a wedding anniversary present by the King. In the winter she liked to have a cheerful blaze of logs burning in her room, and now she was leaving the Palace she wanted her fireplace for her new home. So workmen took it out in its entirety and installed it again in her suite in Clarence House across the Mall. As things turned out, it was not until the beginning of Coronation year that the change-over was complete.

At Clarence House, the move-in went on with much the same atmosphere of sadness. Neither the Queen Mother nor Princess Margaret had much enthusiasm for the job. The Princess, whose life seemed to have been changed completely by her father's death, spent much of her time alone, except when she was helping or comforting her mother. She did not wish to see any of her usual circle of friends, but frequently left the Palace early in the morning with her lady-in-waiting to visit unheralded and privately a church. Happily, both the Queen Mother and Princess Margaret were able later on to throw off this unaccustomed cloak of sadness and revert to their normal lives. Today the Queen Mother is absorbed in her public work, happy in the knowledge that she is carrying on that tradition of service to the people which her husband so firmly established. The Princess, though not quite so gay and lighthearted as of yore, has taken up her familiar pleasures of theater visits, small intimate sherry parties where she and her friends can talk for hours about all sorts of subjects, big and small, and country house weekend visits, interspersed among the many public duties she carries out on behalf of her sister.

CHAPTER ELEVEN

Edward the King

I⊤ was with a general feeling of anxiety that we at Buckingham Palace awaited the coming of the new King, Edward VIII.

From his own bachelor household across the road at York House, St. James's Palace, stories in plenty had come to us about the habits and way of life of the Prince of Wales, which seemed very strange and alien to the sedate well-regulated existence at Buckingham Palace under King George V, when everything had to run with clockwork precision and regularity.

We knew that the Prince was a great stickler for discipline among his officials and servants, and that he always expected a great deal from those who served him. In very striking contrast to the exact timekeeping of his father, the Prince, we knew, regarded time as his slave, and not his master. I remember, when I first went to the Palace, being told by one of the old servants who had joined in Queen Victoria's time that you could set your watch by the King—by which he meant that King George led so regular a life, and paid so much attention to "the courtesy of kings," that he was punctual for every appointment, at home or outside, to the very minute.

Indeed, I tested this story for myself and found that when

the short, immaculately dressed figure of the King came in sight in the Grand Hall on a Tuesday morning, his "stamp day," it was invariably fourteen minutes past ten o'clock. He was on his way from his private rooms on the northeast side of the Palace to the room on the other side where his great and immensely valuable collection of stamps was kept. Stamp Day was an important event of the week for the King. He was passionately interested in his collection, amassed over many years, and comprising the finest and most complete collection of stamps of the British Empire in the world. He would spend the whole day in his Stamp Room, mostly alone, but sometimes with the Keeper of his Philatelic Collection, Sir Edward Bacon, examining, classifying, arranging, and cataloguing his stamps. No State business of an ordinary nature was allowed to disturb him, nor were his family permitted to approach him, except in unusually great emergencies, and then only at the risk of kindling King George's formidable anger and bringing down on their heads a torrent of complaint couched in the emphatic language which he had learned as a young naval officer. He took his lunch and tea in the Stamp Room so as to be able to devote his whole attention to his hobby without interruption.

When I first ventured to time his arrival, therefore, I was not surprised to find him so punctual on this particular day. I quickly learned, however, that the same exact punctuality extended to every movement in his well-ordered life—and woe betide anyone, of Royal blood or not, who dared to keep the King waiting.

With this background of exact timekeeping, it was difficult for us to understand how life could go on at York House, where, according to our friends in the Prince's service, even mealtimes were very elastic, and a lunch ordered for 1:15 might not be eaten until, perhaps, half-past two. There were tales, too, of how the Prince, with his own disregard for time, expected his household and staff to be equally free from conventional regard for the clock. This operated in a difficult way for the servants at York House. They were expected to be ready for duty at any hour day and night, though, they told us, the Prince was very considerate if any of them complained of overwork. He would give them time off, and none of them seemed to mind very much, because of the gift he possessed, in a very marked degree, of commanding intense personal loyalty and affection from those who came into close contact with him. But he suffered from insomnia, which caused him to be fonder of late parties at restaurants and night clubs than he might otherwise have been. It was nothing unusual for him to come back to York House at one, two, or three in the morning, bringing a party of half a dozen gay friends with him. Then the bell would ring and the Prince would order sandwiches and drinks to be served and often a pot of tea for himself. It all sounded very alarming and upsetting to us as we waited for him to come to the Palace.

Each of us received a printed form from the Keeper of the Privy Purse telling us that our contracts had terminated on the death of our employer, King George V, and that we were all under six months' notice. This upset me more than any of the rumors and stories I had heard, but I was assured that it was merely the normal procedure after the death of a Sovereign, and that I had nothing to worry about. This was perfectly true, for the same thing happened sixteen years later at the death of King George VI. But it was not long before our uneasy feelings were justified. Sir Ulick Alexander, Keeper of the Privy Purse, had the unpleasant duty of telling everyone in the Royal service, from the high officers of the Household down to the humblest footman and charwoman, that the King had ordered a 10 per cent cut in all our salaries. Apart from changes in the Household among those working personally with him, and among the servants directly attendant on him, the new King did not want to change the personnel who had served his father so long and so well, we were told, but he was determined to cut down the expenses of running the Palace, which he was sure were too great.

This news came as something of a bombshell to all of us, but there was nothing to do if you wanted to stay at the Palace but to accept.

"It's a bad beginning, my boy," I remember one official of the Household who, like several of his colleagues, did not attempt to disguise in private his disapproval of some of the new King's ways, telling me. "And it will be a bad ending." I had no idea then, in the first few months of what we all hoped would be a long and happy reign, how soon and how dramatically his prophecy would be fulfilled.

After the death of King George V, the Palace was soon very full with visiting foreign Royalty who had come to attend the funeral. Those were still the spacious days of Royalty, when there were many more crowned heads on the thrones of Europe than was the case when King George VI died. Visiting Royalty, too, then traveled in greater state with larger suites of attendants and servants, and it was difficult to find rooms for them all at the Palace. We heard that the King disapproved strongly of all the official entertaining which he was called on to do for the funeral, and he gave a very good example of the firmness with which he could deal with tradition, by canceling the banquet which it had always been customary for the new Sovereign to give at Buckingham Palace to his foreign guests immediately after the funeral of his predecessor.

The incident of the falling Crown, which occurred when King Edward VIII was walking behind the gun carriage carrying his father's body from King's Cross Station to West-minster Hall for the lying-in state, was repeatedly recounted in the Palace corridors and offices as an omen of bad things to come.

It was not for several weeks after his succession that King Edward took up residence at the Palace. He was reluctant, we heard, to leave the snug comfort of his bachelor quarters at York House for the more imposing grandeur of the Palace, just as some years before he had firmly and successfully re-sisted a plan to oust him from St. James's Palace to set up a bigger household at Marlborough House. This time he knew the move would have to be made, but his mother, Queen Mary, had a mass of possessions at the Palace—furniture, pic-tures, antiques, souvenirs of her journeys with King George, and many other belongings—all of which had to be sorted out and separated from the items belonging to the State col-lections. King Edward told his mother there was no hurry whatever, and that she was to take as much time as she wished over her sad task while Marlborough House was being got ready for her occupation.

From time to time we had visits from the King. He would suddenly appear in the kitchens, the cellars, and the store-rooms, or other "behind the scenes" parts of the Palace, walk-ing round, alone, or with one equerry, on tours of inspection. It was all very informal, and quite unlike anything we had seen King George V do at the Palace.

The King asked most businesslike questions in every de-partment, to the surprise, and sometimes dismay, of some of the older members of the staff, who did not expect their King to know anything about the day-to-day domestic details of running the Palace and were not always quite ready with their answers. This, it was easy to see, displeased the King who, as we had been told in advance, was apt to be impatient with anyone who could not give all the answers about his job immediately.

For the first six months of his reign the King gave no formal entertainments, as this was the period of Court mourning, three months shorter than that ordered by his father for Edward VII—another indication of the innovations which the new King Edward was bringing into Court affairs. Of course the King continued to see a good deal of his close friends during this period, though he cut out completely his restaurant and night-club visits.

It was very early indeed in his reign that we at the Palace first became conscious of the importance in the King's scheme of things of Fort Belvedere, the country house in the grounds of Windsor Castle, which his father had given him as a home of his own. One Friday evening in February, 1936, there was a knock on the door of my office just after 6 P.M., and Mr. Williams, my friend the Superintendent of the Palace (his son has succeeded him in the position now), put his head round the door to say, "The King is here."

I uttered a silent prayer of thanks that I had had the sense to stay on in case I was wanted, as we had all been warned that as long as the King was in the Palace any of us might be sent for at any time of the day or night.

The King walked in, his bowler hat in his hand, wearing his heavy fur-lined coat. At once he began to give me orders to send foodstuffs down "to the Fort"—a phrase with which we all became very familiar in the coming months. As usual, the King was driving down to his Windsor home for the weekend. It was a pleasure indeed to take his clear and precise instructions. He knew exactly what he wanted, and told me how many people would be there.

This was my first experience of taking such orders direct from the King and, again, it seemed very strange to me, when he had so many people at his beck and call, that he should trouble to attend to the small details himself. But I quickly learned that he regarded Fort Belvedere very much as a private house, and himself, when there, as a private gentleman. The King would have as many as twenty guests to cold supper at the Fort. Supplies of cold beef—one of his own favorite dishes—with salads and quantities of fruit, peaches, grapes, apricots, pears, and figs, would be sent down in hampers in one of the Palace shooting brakes to his housekeeper, Mrs. Johnson.

After the King had moved into Buckingham Palace, the French Pastry Chef, M. André Rous, prepared for him as a luncheon sweet the Danish dish of Rodgrod, which was originally introduced to the Palace by Queen Alexandra. This sweet, which is made of the juice of crushed raspberries and red currants and ground rice, is still served at Buckingham Palace, where today it is a great favorite with Prince Charles and Princess Anne. King Edward, who had not apparently eaten the dish since his childhood days, when he used to lunch with his grandmother, was delighted to taste it again. That Friday, making what we had come to know as his usual evening call at my office, he asked us to provide him with the recipe for the dish, so that his own cook at the Fort could prepare it.

He was always interested, even in his younger days as Prince of Wales, in special dishes and rare foods. I well remember the commotion he caused at Sandringham at Christmas in 1935, when he came along to my office, his face aglow with enthusiasm, to tell us, "I want to give the King and Queen a special surprise tonight at dinner. Please get a dozen of the finest avocado pears, and let me know personally when they have arrived." With that, the Prince went off, leaving me to wonder exactly how and where I could procure this delicacy in the wilds of Norfolk, the day after Boxing Day. Thanks to my hotel training, I knew what they were. I got on the telephone to two of our fruiterers in London but neither could supply the pears. Then I telephoned a big fruiterer at Victoria. Yes, they had eighteen, and I asked them to send them at once. During the next few hours I had several calls from the impatient Prince to ask when, if ever, his order was to be carried out. When the precious fruit arrived in the shooting brake I had dispatched to meet the London train, I sent him a message to this effect. Within a couple of minutes I heard his footsteps in the corridor. "Got them? Good man!" he said.

Behind him came Princess Alice, Countess of Athlone, wife of Queen Mary's brother, the Earl of Athlone, and always a great favorite with us on the staff because of her keen sense of humor. She was staying as a member of the Christmas house party, and, familiar with avocados from her days in South Africa, was anxious to see what her nephew proposed to do with them. The Prince, in a gray lounge suit, picked up a knife and began to open one of the pears to see if it was ripe. He and his aunt shared the fruit, eating it with spoons.

"We'll eat them with a vinegar and oil dressing at dinner as a first course," the Prince told me. "But don't let the Chef or anyone spoil the surprise by telling what we are going to have."

King George V had spent most of the day before in bed. He was up that day, however, and had announced his intention of staying up to dinner. Servants waiting at the Royal table that night told us how the King had picked up one of the green fruits, inquiring, "What in heaven's name is this? Dessert at the start of the meal?" When the Prince explained it was his idea, his father commented, in gruff humor, "Another of David's mad tricks." Unperturbed, the Prince showed his father and mother how to eat the fruit, pouring an oil and vinegar French salad dressing over the fruit after cutting it in half and removing the stone. Queen Mary seemed to enjoy the novel dish greatly, certainly more than the King, whose tastes in food were ultra conservative. I was never again asked to obtain avocado pears for the Royal menus.

The State functions of the new reign began to take up the King's attention. At St. James's Palace he held morning Levees. On these occasions the King, in full-dress service uniform as a Field Marshal, Admiral of the Fleet, or a Marshal of the Royal Air Force, would drive over in state to St. James's in the Irish Coach (made for Queen Victoria when she visited Dublin in 1900), and in the State Rooms would stand on the throne dais while officers of the Services and others were presented to him with great ceremony and formality. These picturesque functions have not been held since before the war, because King George VI and Queen Elizabeth II have wished to spare men the unnecessary expense of buying or hiring full-dress uniform.

In June the King gave two presentation garden parties at the Palace which ranked for ladies in place of the evening Courts which the King was reluctant to hold as a bachelor without a consort. These parties were run on the familiar lines of the Royal garden parties which had always been a feature of his father's reign. But now came a garden party of a different kind, yet another, and even more striking, illustration of the new King's attitude. He had given orders to the Lord Chamberlain to arrange a special party in the Palace gardens for a big party of Canadian war veterans who had crossed the Atlantic to attend the unveiling of the memorial to their fallen comrades at Vimy Ridge in France. King Edward, to whom his experiences in the trenches remained always most vivid, had himself crossed to France to unveil the memorial, and now he invited his old comrades to visit him in his home at the Palace.

It was a remarkable sight to the conservative-minded officials of the Court to see the Canadians strolling around the Palace grounds and passing through the famous Bow Saloon between the lovely collections of English and foreign porcelain, dressed in lounge suits, all wearing their war medals, and many of them with berets on their heads. It was in striking contrast with the usual elegant, morning-coated, top-hatted guests at the normal Palace garden parties. Tea was served in the gardens and then with that bad luck which, looking back, so often dogged many of King Edward's public functions, it rained very hard.

The King, strolling through the throngs of his Canadian guests, turned to go into the Palace. The party on which he had set such store was in danger of turning into a fiasco. King Edward, however, always had ideas of his own for dealing with any situation. With a word to two or three of his staff, he hurried indoors and went up to the Music Room on the first floor. A minute or two later his familiar figure, bareheaded in the rain, appeared on the balcony, and to the surprise of everyone, Court officials and guests alike, the King made a short, characteristically warmhearted speech of welcome, ending with regrets that the weather had let them down. Never before in the memory of the oldest member of the Royal Household had a Sovereign spoken so informally and without advance notice or preparation of any kind to a gathering such as this at a garden party at the Palace. Opinion was sharply divided afterward as the Househlod and officials discussed the speech. The older ones, naturally, were taken aback by this new example of the changes that were taking place in Royal procedure. The younger ones among us took the view that this was a fine thing—as everyone today will agree it was—for the King to step down for a moment from his exalted isolation and talk almost as man to man to the men who had been under fire with him in the muddy trenches of France and Flanders. Certainly there was no shadow of a doubt about what the Canadians felt. No cheers throughout his eleven-month reign sounded more sincere and enthusiastic than those with which the Canadians greeted his speech.

It was after the King had returned to the Palace from re-viewing his Household Troops in Hyde Park that we all ad-mired him most. As he led the columns of soldiers down Constitution Hill, mounted on his charger, a man suddenly appeared in his path, brandishing a revolver, which he hurled at the King. An equerry rushed from the King's side to deal with the man, but the King, quite unperturbed, rode on as though nothing had happened. In the forecourt of the Palace I watched him in his high bearskin and scarlet tunic, as Colonel-in-Chief of the Grenadier Guards, sit with absolute composure astride his horse as he turned it toward the en-trance to the King's Door. There was nothing in his bearing or demeanor to show that only a few minutes earlier he had been exposed to what looked like an attempt at an assassi-nation.

One feature of Palace life under Edward VIII, unique in my experience, was that unexpected orders were always being given. No one, from the Private Secretary downward, quite knew what was going to happen next, or what the King would be doing tomorrow. In a way it was quite a refreshing change after the rigidly fixed timetable of King George V's day, when you could predict with absolute certainty the movements of the King and Queen several months, indeed, a year ahead. But some people, apparently in the know, seemed to have grave doubts about whether this was the way the Palace should be run. Only two people, Inspector David Storrier, the King's personal police officer who had been with him for several years as Prince, and Mr. George Ladbrook, his chauffeur for many years, ever seemed to know anything definite about his movements in advance.

Orders in July were very surprising. The King was to go for a holiday cruise in the Adriatic in a borrowed yacht, the *Nahlin,* with a party of friends. Among the names on the list circulated at the Palace was that of Mrs. Ernest Simpson. This was a name already well known to us within the Palace. We sometimes saw her with him in the Palace gardens, slim, dark-haired, and extremely well dressed. Everyone knew she had been a close friend of his for some time. Nor was the guest list for the *Nahlin* the first occasion on which we had read her name. One day, while the King was still living at York House, he sent across a list of names of his guests at a dinner party for publication in the Court Circular the next day. There was a great deal of quiet comment inside the Palace when we saw the names of Major and Mrs. Ernest Simpson, the King's private friends, alongside those of official guests like Lord and Lady Wigram, and members of the Government.

This was the first open indication of the King's friendship for the American lady for whom he was destined to renounce the throne. Now she, without her husband, was to be his guest on the yachting cruise. Tongues wagged freely in the Palace from then onward. Before the *Nahlin*'s departure we were all wondering what was to happen at Balmoral, where, for the first time almost since the beginning of the century, the Royal Standard was not flying in the first weeks of August. When the King came back we heard. The King was going to Balmoral in mid-September for a twelve-day stay—the shortest on record. In this trip, too, Mrs. Simpson, with two of her friends, Mr. and Mrs. Herman Rogers, was again to be the King's guest.

Up in the Highlands little serious notice had, up to now, been taken about the gossip in London, but the conservative Aberdonians and Deesiders were astonished when the King hurried out of the Royal train at Aberdeen to complete the journey to Balmoral in a large American black Buick car instead of by train, when he would have been met formally by the Lord Lieutenant, the Marquess of Aberdeen, at Ballater Station, like his father before him. The King's Buick, which he nearly always used for his weekend rides to the Fort, was, unlike the State Daimlers, built with a tiny rear window which made it virtually impossible to see anyone traveling in it. But the story quickly spread throughout Deeside that it was Mrs. Simpson who was the King's companion on the journey to Balmoral. She was not, in fact, with him in the car!

There were about twenty guests at Balmoral, including the King's favorite brother, the Duke of Kent. Outwardly everything went on as in previous years. The King arranged grouse shooting on the moors, late though it was. There were stalking parties, too, and, to the great delight of the ghillies, the King himself went out stalking several times. It is true that he disappointed them once or twice by taking nothing more lethal than a cine-camera with which to "shoot" the stags.

In the evening the procedure seemed, on the surface, practically the same as in the days of King George V. When the guns came in there was tea, and after an interval for baths and changing, there were cocktails or sherry before dinner, with a film show afterward in the ballroom. But there were great differences in fact. Dinner, hitherto always served precisely at 8:30, was now ordered for 9:30 P.M., and sometimes served fifteen minutes or more late. After dinner the King's Pipers played around the table, as they had done in the previous reigns, so the film was late in starting. Nor was this all. After the film each night there would be an order brought down by the King's Page for hot club sandwiches for twenty-five or thirty, to be sent up to the drawing room on silver dishes. Sometimes there was a further order, and it would be 2 or 3 A.M. before King Edward and his guests retired. After a few nights of this and a good deal of grumbling, I arranged for a second chef to do late night duty—the only practicable solution to this problem.

It was part of my job at Balmoral to type out the Court Circular with the names of the King's guests which, on his personal orders, were included as they arrived and departed. But I little imagined what excitement and sensation would be caused by the Circular in which I typed the name of Mrs. Ernest Simpson. Deeside was ablaze with gossip the following day when it became known that the King had motored the fifty-odd miles into Aberdeen from Balmoral to meet his lady friend and drive her back to Balmoral. But this, officially at any rate, was none of my business.

This visit ended in great sadness for King Edward. His favorite Cairn terrier, which had been with him on the grouse moors the day before he left for London, was lost. Keepers and ghillies scoured the countryside for hours without avail, and the King had to board his train for London not knowing what had happened to the dog. The day after, as I was getting into the train at Ballater on my way back to the Palace, a Castle car pulled up in the station square, and out stepped one of the keepers, holding the little Cairn. He had spent a whole day and night and the next morning on the moors, before being found. On the staff train going south I was able to hand the dog over to a young cook from Fort Belvedere who knew him well. She petted him on the train, and was delighted to be able to deliver him in person to the King when she arrived at Buckingham Palace. Afterward she told me she never remembered seeing the King look so delighted.

None of us knew at that time what was causing the King's sadness, though not long after we had a very ominous indication. A few days after returning from Balmoral, the King, who was extremely restless, was off again, this time to Sandringham. In his Norfolk home he entertained an all-male party for the pheasant and partridge shooting. At this time the famous divorce proceedings in which Mrs. Ernest Simpson obtained a decree against her husband took place at Ipswich.

One morning the King's Page came into my office with a personal order from His Majesty that four of the best pheasants I could find should be put into a parcel for him. The parcel, when packed, was placed in the King's car, which stood outside in the yard. A few minutes later the King, looking more worried than I had ever seen him, came out, hurried into his car, and drove off. A few days later I was told where the pheasants had gone. The King had taken them personally to deliver them to Mrs. Simpson.

It was not long after this that the King made known his intention of marrying Mrs. Simpson, thus provoking the constitutional crisis that resulted in his Abdication.

CHAPTER TWELVE

Another Royal Romance:
Princess Margaret and Peter Townsend

MY POSITION in the Royal Household enabled me to observe at close hand the growth of another Royal romance,
that between Princess Margaret and Group Captain Peter
Townsend. The Group Captain, picked by the King as an
equerry of honor in 1944, became so popular with the Royal
Family that he was retained by the King as a permanent
equerry at the Palace. When the Royal Family went to South
Africa in 1947, Group Captain Peter Townsend went with
them as Acting Master of the Household for the trip. So well
did he acquit himself on this task that when he came back
he was made Deputy Master of the Household by the King.
In this position I came into daily and close contact with him
as Deputy Comptroller of Supply and worked very closely
indeed with the Group Captain.

There has never been any doubt in my mind that these two
young people were in love.

The dashing young Group Captain, then a Wing Commander with the Distinguished Flying Cross, and Bar, and
the Distinguished Service Order, won in the Battle of Britain,
made a tremendous impression on the fourteen-year-old Princess Margaret when he first came onto her father's staff. As

the years went by the friendship and affection between them grew, coming to a head, I have been told, in South Africa, where they used to go for rides together along the shore by the Indian Ocean.

I know that when they came back there was a definite look in Princess Margaret's eyes whenever she caught sight of the handsome black-haired young Group Captain. She always had a smile for him and he always had one for her.

The Group Captain was "Peter" to the late King, to the Queen Mother, to the Queen, to other members of the Royal Family including Princess Margaret, but there always seemed to me to be a special quality of affection about the way Princess Margaret pronounced that name "Peter" and similarly an affectionate quality, though tempered with deep respect, in the way he addressed her as "Princess."

They became very close to each other indeed in the last two years that I was at the Palace. Wherever the Court might be, in Scotland, in Norfolk, or in Berkshire, the Group Captain was always sure to be included in the house party at some stage of the Royal stay if Princess Margaret was there. I found it most amusing in those days to read and to hear of the Princess's name being linked with this young man or that young man, various officers of the Guards and scions of the nobility who all of them in turn had been invited to join the Royal party at one house or another. I have seen them all come—and go away to wed some other lady or to stay bachelors. People like the Marquess of Blandford, the Earl of Dalkeith, and many others. Always the Group Captain would be among the party, quite content to let the limelight of publicity shine on these other young men, doing his best to help make them happy and comfortable throughout their stay. But to those of us in the background there was never any doubt whatever as to whom the Princess wanted to sit near her during an after-dinner film show in one of the private cinemas at the Royal residences. It was always Peter.

I sat close behind the Royal Family at these cinema shows. I delighted in the rather ceremonious way in which the Royal Family would walk in, headed by the King and the Queen Mother, followed by the two Princesses and the young men of the party. When the King had taken his seat with his Queen beside him, the others would take their seats to the left and right of the Royal couple in the same row and proceed to fill up the rows of chairs behind. Princess Margaret would nearly always take a seat behind the front or second row and keep a chair next to her for the Group Captain who waited rather quietly until the King would call for the lights to go out. Then the Group Captain would slip silently in to take his seat beside Princess Margaret, placing a rug about her knees if it was cold, and putting out an ash tray for her cigarette and holder. There was a definite atmosphere of contentment between the two as they would settle down to watch the film.

I always thought, "Good luck to them." It used to amuse me a good deal on these occasions to observe the disapproval being expressed among older members of the Household toward the Group Captain for his manners with the Princess. But that was the way the Princess wanted it; she was happy and so was he.

It was at Balmoral that I received my really firm impression of the affection between the two. This was back in 1952. I was working with the Group Captain planning a small dance. I wanted some information and instructions from him so I left my office to look for him in the billiard room which adjoins the Tower Door entrance to Balmoral Castle. Not finding him there, I asked a footman to tell me where he was and went in search of him toward the lounge, down a long carpeted corridor which leads past the Royal dining room toward the front entrance. As I was going along I almost bumped into the Group Captain and Princess Margaret. She was coming down the stairs from her rooms and he was at the bottom of the stairs talking up to her.

She looked radiant and happy in her Highland dress and was merrily in conversation with him. I asked Her Royal Highness to excuse me while I spoke to the Group Captain about my business. She nodded her assent and permission and stood on one side listening, smiling happily at me as I spoke to Peter.

I had heard all the rumors, all the chitchat between the Servants' Hall and the Steward's Room and the officials' mess. I had seen the Princess and the Group Captain together in the ballroom, walking out in the grounds, riding together in the woods, sitting together in the cinema, but this time I knew the rumors were right. It is difficult, almost impossible, to define such an atmosphere, but the Princess seemed to me to be smiling at me as if to say, "You understand." I have rarely seen two people look happier together.

The Group Captain is intelligent, businesslike, immaculate in dress and manner, a good ladies' man at parties, a first-class pilot who has flown planes for the Princess in the King's Cup Air Race, and a very good shot. On the Scottish moors I have seen him hold his own with other much more experienced shots at the grouse butts and I have seen him, too, go out on the hills after deer, knocking down a stag with the best of them. I always liked working with Peter Townsend. He was of the younger generation at Court, a few years younger than I myself, and I found it very refreshing to work with him after some of the older officials with their love for precedents, which sometimes made them take several hours to decide some quite simple point of procedure.

A small personal memory I have and shall always cherish of Peter Townsend comes from the year 1946 when the Court was in residence at Balmoral Castle. Group Captain Townsend was not among the original Castle party. The King summoned him to join the Household in a great hurry and when he arrived he found he had left home without packing his dinner jacket. At Balmoral, as I have said elsewhere, members of the Royal Household lunch and dine with the Royal Family and therefore it was essential for Peter Townsend to be properly garbed with a black tie and a dinner jacket when he went to dine with the King and Queen in the evening. He came to tell me his trouble and I was very delighted to be able to loan him my own dinner clothes. He wore them every evening and I had a certain amount of quiet amusement to think that the dinner jacket and trousers and black tie of the humble Freddie Corbitt were on parade at the Royal dining table each night.

But I was not so pleased one night when General Eisenhower and his wife, who were staying at the Castle for a weekend visit, went to dine with the King and Queen and afterward attended a dance in the ballroom. Group Captain Peter Townsend, of course, was among the party and, equally of course, he wore my dinner jacket. This did not worry me at dinnertime, but afterward when the dance came on I was worried. It was part of my duty to be present in the ballroom to keep an eye on the general goings-on and to see that refreshments were served. But without a dinner jacket I could not appear within sight of the Royal Family.

So I had to hide myself in a lounge suit tucked away at the other end of the room, watching out to see what was going on in the distance, while the Group Captain sat on the dais with the King and Queen and General Eisenhower and his wife and their friends. The program that night included the

Scottish dances the Eightsome Reel, the Dashing White Sergeant, and the Circassian Circle. Mrs. Eisenhower joined in the dancing with the King, but the General, I remember, smiled and shook his head. "I prefer to keep a watching brief," he commented, and spent the evening sitting on the Royal dais observing the changing scene.

From her girlhood Princess Margaret always has had a great attraction for the opposite sex. When she was still in her early teens during the war years Princess Margaret, then living with her sister at Windsor Castle—the "house in the country" which was referred to so often in the newspaper reports about the Royal Family without ever being mentioned by name, for security reasons—was fond, as any normal girl of her age will be, of the company of young men.

She was always ready for adventure. I remember very well on V-E night, May 8, 1945, when the crowds were packed in milling thousands outside the Palace, it was Princess Margaret who, nudging her sister by the arm, suggested that they should go down and see the Palace from the outside instead of watching the crowds from the Palace balcony. Princess Elizabeth, always conscious of her sense of duty, said that she would be delighted to go out but they had better ask "Daddy." The King was asked and readily gave his consent, adding with a smile to his two daughters, "Be careful you don't get lost."

A few moments later the two Princesses with loose coats slung over their shoulders, accompanied by two of the young equerries, slipped down the corridor along to the lift and so down to the ground floor. They passed along the red-carpeted corridor in the front of the Palace through a side door and into the stone-flagged servants' corridor which led them to the Trade Gate. With the Palace police in ignorance of their movements the two Princesses and their escorts slipped out into the crowds outside. Within a few moments they were lost to view.

"Just like Princess Margaret—she loves an adventure," commented an old Royal servant who watched the two girls disappear into the crowds.

It was nearly an hour later that the two Princesses returned, a little disheveled, laughing, their faces flushed and delighted with their entirely novel experience. Few of the people who had rubbed shoulders with them in those cheering crowds, delighted with victory and the end of the war in Europe, realized that it was with their future Queen and her sister that they had been on such close terms.

This was a harmless adventure enough, but it is impossible for anyone who knows the Queen to imagine her starting it. It was the impish delight of Princess Margaret, always eager to do something that she had not done before, to try the new road that led the two sisters onto this pleasant little adventure.

Like any other attractive girl of rank and position, Princess Margaret had her beaux in hundreds, or at least in scores, during her teens. Young Guards officers, the sons of her father's friends, Peers, commoners, and many others of all ranks and positions came to Buckingham Palace, to Windsor Castle, to Royal Lodge, or to Sandringham, eager to further their acquaintance with the King's attractive younger daughter.

And attractive indeed Princess Margaret was. Very small of stature, slight of build, with tiny bones, Princess Margaret was an elfin little Princess. Her coloring was exquisite; her large blue eyes full of intelligence and charm. Her voice, strikingly like that of her mother, was calculated to charm anyone when she spoke to him.

When she sang, as she so often did in those days, to her

own accompaniment at the piano, it was a delight to listen to her. Many times as I have passed along the corridors of Buckingham Palace I have stopped, entranced, to hear the Princess's clear young voice ringing out in melody to the accompaniment of her own playing. She loved to play French nursery rhymes and other French country songs that she had learned as a little girl, as well as sophisticated numbers which she used to learn from records specially flown over to her from the United States.

King George VI and Queen Elizabeth tried very hard never to show any favoritism between their two daughters. Princess Elizabeth, however, was close to her father on affairs of State. He always regarded her, of course, as his eventual successor and took enormous pains to train her for the arduous job of Queen-ship.

For his other daughter, whose future was unclouded with the thought of a throne ahead, the King had a tender affection. With her he could have a gayer time because there was never a question of State affairs to discuss between them.

Queen Elizabeth, too, seemed to have a specially soft spot always in her heart for her younger daughter.

In those days, when her father was still alive, Princess Margaret was a very gay young person indeed. She loved to entertain, and in her own room on the second floor of Buckingham Palace—in that part of the front of the Palace which is now the Royal nursery for Prince Charles and Princess Anne—she would give little parties for her friends.

The Princess's Circle, as they became known, numbered some of the most intelligent and amusing young men and young women in the top social strata of London. These young men and women would call at the Palace and be taken up to the Princess's room. Here there would be sherry, biscuits, sandwiches, and cocktails served. There was always also a plentiful supply of cigarettes. Princess Margaret was the heaviest smoker of all the Royal Family and she was always keen that her guests should have a good supply of cigarettes as well.

Princess Margaret's own preference in the matter of drinks was always for gin and angostura bitters, which she drank with a good deal of water. I have seen her also drink champagne but she was not ever very fond of alcohol.

Miss Sharman Douglas, daughter of the American Ambassador of those days, was a close friend of Princess Margaret. The two girls saw life from much the same angle, and the Princess was delighted with the wider experience of her American friend. It was Sharman Douglas and Princess Margaret who between them evolved the idea of the famous "cancan" dance at a party at the American Embassy which subsequently shocked some of the more narrow-minded.

On this, as on nearly every other occasion, Princess Margaret took the precaution of asking her parents' consent before she carried out her intention. The Queen had told her daughter that there could be no possible harm in her dancing the "cancan" after she had seen the very modified version of the famous French dance which the Princess and her friends proposed to do. When there was some public outcry afterward, Princess Margaret was secure in the knowledge that her mother and father had known all the while what she was going to do and had given their approval.

But it was not always approval that the Princess found from her father, in particular. I well remember an occasion when the Court was in residence at Holyroodhouse in Edinburgh and there was a garden party to the Scottish nobility and gentry. The King, in Highland dress, with Queen Elizabeth, at his side, were walking through the gardens in a dignified and solemn manner befitting the spirit of Edinburgh, talking gravely to some of the leading citizens of the second Kingdom, when Princess Margaret made her appearance in the garden coming out through a side door of the Palace.

There were some looks, if not expressions, of surprise on the faces of some of the Scottish ladies. Princess Margaret had for the afternoon chosen a particularly vivid shade of lipstick and rouge, giving her a much over-painted appearance, though in fact she had not an excess of make-up on. But among the Scottish ladies, most of whom had no make-up at all, the Princess stood out.

When she joined her parents, the King took one glance at his daughter and his face, too, set in lines of stern disapproval.

This was an occasion when Princess Margaret—she was then sixteen—had gone just one step too far. It was some weeks before the King finally forgave her and for many months afterward there was a good deal of chaffing and leg-pulling in the Royal Family about the day Margaret "put on the lot."

All this time the innocent friendship between Peter Townsend and the Princess was growing. Gradually it ripened into something much deeper and more binding.

When the Royal Family came back from their tour of South Africa in May, 1947, all the public attention was focused upon Princess Elizabeth, whose engagement to the handsome Prince Philip of Greece and Denmark, as he had been—by this time he was plain Lieutenant Philip Mountbatten, R.N., a naturalized British subject—and few people took very much notice of the younger Princess. This delighted Princess Margaret and allowed her full scope to lead her own life.

Princess Margaret and the Queen were very close as girls, and Princess Margaret felt the separation keenly when her sister left to take up her residence at Clarence House as a married woman. The well-known story—and it is a true one—of how Princess Margaret made the comment at the birth of Prince Charles, "Now I shall be known as Charlie's Aunt," has something more to it than just a laugh. I think it was a way of expressing Princess Margaret's feeling of loneliness. Once her sister had left to take up her married life, Princess Margaret was really alone at Buckingham Palace with no one to whom she could talk as an equal. In this gap in her life Group Captain Peter Townsend filled an increasingly important place. They seemed to have the same ideas, the same interests and to talk the same language. Daily they were in each other's company in the afternoons when the Court was at Buckingham Palace. Whether the King and Queen were in residence in London or in the country, nearly every afternoon the Group Captain would spend an hour or more with the Princess, giving her lessons in elocution. He has an extremely good speaking voice and the Princess, when she began to appear in public life, found that she had inherited some of her father's nervousness in the way of speaking. Peter Townsend helped to cure her of this, so that today she is a very accomplished speaker.

But the close feelings between them really became apparent just after King George VI's death. Princess Margaret was bewildered and devastated at the loss of her dearly loved father. Though she, like other members of the Royal Family, had known for at least two years that the end might be sudden and was inevitable, when it came it took her by surprise. On that sad February morning at Sandringham there was no one in the Royal Household more distraught than Princess Margaret. Pale, thin, with heavy lines under her eyes, she was in great sorrow. From this time, Princess Margaret gave up her gay life and her young friends and took to going to church regularly. When the Court came back to London after the Queen's accession, the Princess would slip out time and again, accompanied only by a lady-in-waiting, to go to St. Peter's Church in Eaton Square to take early Communion. Again in the evening she would leave Buckingham Palace by a side door and go to church to say her prayers in privacy.

So devoted did the Princess become in those days to her religion that the rumor went round Buckingham Palace and spread outside the Palace gates that she would take the veil and go into a convent. There was never the slightest foundation for this story.

It is not, perhaps, without significance that Group Captain Townsend himself is a very religious man. In the last two or three years of his stay at Buckingham Palace he was often to be found with a Bible in his hand, reading quietly to himself.

There was never any question while King George VI was alive but that he and his Queen knew that the affection between Princess Margaret and Group Captain Peter Townsend was developing. They took no steps that I ever heard of to stop it, so it is to be inferred that they felt that Princess Margaret, if she was determined to find her happiness with him, should be allowed to do so.

It is certain that when King George VI died, his widow asked Peter Townsend to go over with her to Clarence House to be either Comptroller of her Household or Master of her Household. A suite of rooms was prepared for him at Clarence House.

I sometimes wonder what King George VI would have done if, when he summoned the young Wing Commander with his war decorations to Windsor Castle back on that spring morning in 1944, he had known what was going to happen. Would he have asked Peter Townsend to stay, or would he have told him that there was no job for him at Buckingham Palace? I think that King George VI, with his devotion to his daughter's happiness, would probably have weighed the matter up and kept Townsend at the Palace. If otherwise, why did King George VI not send Peter Townsend away years ago, when the friendship between him and Princess Margaret was really developing into something warmer? Perhaps he and Queen Elizabeth hoped that this was a girlish fancy which would quickly pass. If so, they underrated the strength of feeling of their younger daughter. In my view she never wavered in her affection for Peter Townsend over several years.

CHAPTER THIRTEEN

The Ever-Changing, Ever-Stable Monarchy

Today, as I look back over my long years at Buckingham Palace, and review the changes I saw there from the inside, and the others I have watched from outside the Palace walls, I can detect a definite pattern in the evolution of the Monarchy.

The four Sovereigns under whom I served have all wrought changes in the life of the Court, have all reshaped, in greater or less degree, the way of life and the machinery of Monarchy left by their predecessors. Small things, like the direct telephone orders of Queen Elizabeth II and the Duke of Edinburgh, and many more I have mentioned in these pages, are the outward signs of the changes I mean, but their importance is far greater than it would seem, for they are merely symbolic of the constantly changing relationship between the Sovereign and the people which is, I think, the mainstay of our wonderful British system of constitutional kingship.

Yet always, the principles remain the same, and the affection and love lavished on the Queen, her husband, and family by all classes is ample proof of the stability of the Monarchy. The members of our Royal Family have, it almost seems, a special kind of genius for adapting themselves to the ever-changing conditions of the world outside the Palace gates, without ever seeming to make any drastic departures from the expected. But the changes are no less definite for emerging gradually. The round-the-world solo trip of the Duke of Edinburgh which was to take him to Australia to open the Olympic Games and keep him out of England for Christmas is proof of that.

To King George V, to spend Christmas anywhere but at his beloved Sandringham would have been anathema, and to spend it separated from his family circle unthinkable, even though, as I have tried to show, the relations between him and his children were not on the same intimate footing as existed between King George VI and his daughters, or as exists today between the Queen and the Duke and their two children. Family Christmas was a very definite part of the Royal calendar, whose various features succeeded each other in an almost ritualistic procession, unalterable, unchangeable.

To the Duke and the Queen, such strict adherence to custom seems unnecessary. They prefer to make circumstances fit their lives rather than live in a restriction of what-was-done-before.

I believe, based on my own observations throughout my time with the Royal Family, that we shall see this tendency continue, and the Royal program for, say, 1966, will look very little like that for this year, even less like those of my early Palace days.

In 1955, the Queen herself wrought a substantial and, to all connected with the Palace, a striking innovation when instead of spending January and February at Sandringham, as her father, grandfather, and great-grandfather did, she set off with the Duke for her historic tour of Nigeria, and lost no time after her return letting it become known that further trips on these lines, perhaps to the Gold Coast and other parts of her Colonial Empire, are likely in the future.

The world has shrunk even since her father's days, and

the Queen and her husband make no secret of their determination to see as much of it as they can, and to be seen by as many of her subjects as possible, by taking advantage of air travel and modern methods of communication. In the olden days, even just before the war, repeated absences of the Sovereign from the country on long-distance journeys would have effectively upset the delicate balance of Royal machinery in the Government of the Realm and the Commonwealth, simply because it would have taken too long physically for the Sovereign to return in case of a suddenly developing crisis. All that is changed by the acceptance of air travel as a safe and normal way of journeying for Royalty, and, of course, there is the other important constitutional change by which Queen Elizabeth II is as much Queen of Canada and Queen of Australia as she is Queen of England. (It is a particular point of correctness at Buckingham Palace that the title Queen of Britain is never used.) This means that in theory, at any rate, there is no reason why the Queen should not pack up and spend six or nine months a year in one of her overseas realms, or even take up residence permanently in one or other of them. That day may come, but, from my own personal knowledge of the Queen, I should say it is unlikely in her lifetime that the Sovereign will desert Buckingham Palace and Windsor Castle except for Empire tours more or less on the lines to which we have been accustomed. These, while in themselves representing a departure from old custom, are really only an extension of the idea of tours-among-the-people begun by George V and Queen Mary nearly forty years ago.

One of the most lasting impressions I retain from my days at the Palace is that the country and the Commonwealth owe a much greater debt to King George VI and Queen Elizabeth, now the Queen Mother, than most people realize. There is no doubt the Abdication of Edward VIII shook the whole foundations of the Monarchy. When his brother came to the throne, more than half-unwillingly, as I have always understood, just a short series of mistakes could have had devastating results. The King, with his Queen always at his side, made none, though we who were near him knew quite well how nervous he so often was in those early days of "putting a foot wrong," as he sometimes expressed it himself.

Day after day, year after year, he went on doing and saying always the right thing, so that when the day came for him to pass on the Crown to his daughter, after literally spending his life in its service, it was a far brighter and more glowing Royal emblem than when he had reluctantly taken it from the hands of his elder brother. Today, if he is able to know what goes on in the high places where he lived and worked, he must be happy indeed at the proud way his beloved "Lilibet" wears that heavy diadem of exalted rank and vast responsibility.

Sometimes, when I walk past the familiar front of Buckingham Palace, I sigh for the old days. The outside world is very different from the everything-just-so world within. But in my new job among the American Forces, I am continually heartened and refreshed by the absorbing interest all these good fellows from the Republic over the sea take in my tales of the British Royal Family, and of the days when it was my job to see that everything was indeed "fit for a King."